0006191

KT-486-172

TBA
(Dan)

B16536

Contemporary
sociology of
the school
General editor
JOHN EGGLESTON

Social control
and education

CONTEMPORARY SOCIOLOGY
OF THE SCHOOL

PAUL BELLABY
The sociology of comprehensive schooling

BRIAN DAVIES
Social control and education

SARA DELAMONT
Interaction in the classroom

JOHN EGGLESTON
The ecology of the school

ERIC HOYLE
School organization and administration

COLIN LACEY
The socialization of teachers

PHILIP ROBINSON
Education and poverty

MICHAEL STUBBS
Language, schools and classrooms

WILLIAM TYLER
The sociology of educational inequality

TOM WHITESIDE
The sociology of educational innovation

BRIAN DAVIES

Social
control
and
education

METHUEN

First published in 1976 by Methuen & Co Ltd
11 New Fetter Lane, London EC4P 4EE
© 1976 Brian Davies
Printed in Great Britain
by Richard Clay (The Chaucer Press), Ltd,
Bungay, Suffolk

ISBN (hardbound) 0 416 55800 3
ISBN (paperback) 0 416 55810 X

CONTENTS

Preface

Sociologists are given endemically to their own species of holy war about the possession of true belief. Groups self-lacerate and snipe at one another and at adjacent parties in the hope of gaining dominance for their own one best way of seeing and explaining human events, when the very nature of experience cries out for a variety of forms of understanding. Man's activity has both subjective and objective dimension, social knowledge is both fact and value. Two or three forms of social explanation in juxtaposition are always better (more complete, less partial) than one. Sociology is not reducible either to politics or morality.

'Social control' sounds like a hard and repressive idea and it can, like any idea, be put to bad use. Does it sound different if we say that the social *is* control? That is the argument of this book, anyway – that what we call freedom and fulfilment is as socially constrained as slavery and alienation. Social control is not some dark opposite to liberation and freedom, it is simply the ubiquitous condition of women and men (and children). One does not choose to live without rules and their

7

consequences, though at times and in some degree it is possible to choose which rules to live with. To know this is to be freer than not to know it, but such freedom may be cold comfort alongside actual experience of some times and places. In this context, education is the more or less systematic pursuit of normalcy in all societies which practise it. It always involves making people more similar as well as more different, but which people, in what degree and to what ends depends upon the nature of a particular society's hierarchy. This and the society's key values or ideologies can be regarded as always being refracted through its educational system. Education is deeply implicated in the processes of generating and transmitting key messages as to knowledge, personal and social realities. Its complexity is largely derivative in relation to these and is great.

The plan of the book hopefully follows the logic of these beliefs. The first chapter attempts to outline a view of key issues in present day sociology. The discipline is in an exciting stage, perhaps even at a point of no return in respect of its historical innocence. There is little but ideological gain in pursuing questions of social control without a good grasp of how we grasp the social, and the social is not exhausted by sociology let alone captured by a single sociological approach. I have tried to encompass as many of these differences as possible in talking about models of men which major social theories work with. This route seemed of special interest if we are to clarify the question of who is controlled, how and why, by what.

As education is a historically complexly arrived at set of social institutions, the next two chapters are then devoted to aspects of the rise of schooling in Britain and the United States. My aim here is to try to reduce the power of simplistic versions of instantly possible change and to suggest the view that many present diagnoses of educational problems miss the point that the problems of mass *education* have not yet been seriously conceptualized, let alone tackled. In explication of these questions, I then return in greater depth to the theoretical and empirical traditions of Marx and Durkheim, both in their own and more recent terms. All this enables us to see more clearly which aspects of education and social control have been elaborated and neglected in main stream sociology of education, down to the present day. The conclusion as to what it is that we know in research terms about what schools do to individuals comes out a bit thin, but that in a sense is only to say that there is a great deal of exciting work to be done, if only we believe that the questions are more than rhetorical.

For helping me to clarify my own questions through varying degrees of encouragement, advice and denial, having read a first draft of the book, my special thanks to Basil Bernstein, Peter Corbishley, John Eggleston, Bob Gough, Gerald Grace, Tony Green, John Hayes, Margaret Jackson, John Mace, Jimmy McGhee, Lyn McGregor, Pat McKenna, John Naylor, Philip Robinson, Lazar Vlasceanu and Michael Young.

Editor's
introduction

In the past decade our understanding of the complexities of societies and their educational arrangements has been transformed. A diverse and ever-growing body of theoretical and empirical research has demonstrated the over-simplification of those earlier sociological views that held the world to be a place that ran smoothly with agreed norms of behaviour, with institutions and individuals performing functions that maintained society, and where conflict was restricted to 'agreed' areas. This normative view of society, dominated by functionalist and conflict theories, has now to be augmented in the light of a range of newer interpretative approaches, in which the realities of human interaction have been explored by phenomenologists, ethnomethodologists and other reflexive theorists. Together they emphasize the part that individual perceptions play in determining social reality, and challenge many of the characteristics of society that earlier sociologists assumed to be 'given'.

The combination of new and long standing approaches has had striking effects upon the sociology of the school. Earlier work was characterized by a range of incompletely examined assumptions about such matters as ability, opportunity and social class. Sociologists asked how working-class schoolchildren could achieve like middle-class schoolchildren. Now they also ask how a social system defines concepts such as class, opportunities and achievement. Such concepts and many others, such as subjects, the curriculum and even schools themselves, are seen to be products of the social system in which they exist. In these approaches to the study of the school we can see with far greater clarity the ways in which individual teachers' and students' definitions of the situation help to determine its social arrangements; how perceptions of achievement cannot only define achievement, but also identify those who achieve; how expectations about schooling can determine the nature and evaluation of schools.

This series of volumes explores the main areas of the sociology of the school in which new understandings of events are available. Each book introduces the reader to the new interpretations, juxtaposes them against the longer-standing perspectives and reappraises the contemporary practice of education and its consequences. The authors in the series have worked extensively in their areas of specialism and have been encouraged not only to introduce the reader to their subject but also to develop, where appropriate, their own analyses of the issues. Yet though each volume has its distinctive, critical approach, the themes and treatments of all of them are closely interrelated. The series as a whole is offered to all who seek understanding of the practice of education in present-day societies, and to those who wish to know how contemporary sociological theory may be applied to the educational issues of those societies.

In *Social Control and Education* Brian Davies explores a whole range of enthusiasms which have passed for 'new sociologies' including the current vogue for seeing the school as 're-producer' of society's existing stratification, power and value systems. He argues that a satisfactory grasp of varying approaches to social control presupposes an understanding of the models or images of man which are embedded in irreducibly differing social theories. The first part of his book constitutes a perceptive and provocative tour of these models. He goes on to consider the rise of schooling in Britain and North America, demonstrating the complex but often incompletely visible ways in which it is defined what knowledge should be available, to whom it shall be available and to which areas high or low status be accorded; and the implications of these processes for the power and authority structure of societies. The argument, though necessarily detailed, is presented with remarkable liveliness and humour and an equally notable justice and sensitivity. It constitutes an original, important, and accessible new contribution to our understanding of education in modern societies.

John Eggleston

1

Background: basic issues in sociology

Agreement more apparent than real?

Facing up to writing a short book entitled *Social Control and Education* involves the realization that one has undertaken a task rather akin to whistling the Messiah, solo, in the Albert Hall in no more than eleven minutes, flat. The range of material to be covered is potentially immense but, unlike great works of art, parts of it stand in unwieldy relationship to others. The very term 'social control' has a different origin and history in sociology and has long meant very different things to different sorts of sociologists. In this sense, of course, it is by no means unique in social science, where almost every basic concept has a multi-meaning character. But it is as well to grasp this fact straight away and recognize that in consequence of it we shall have to spend a fair bit of space clarifying what sociologists mean by social control, as well as how they write about education.

Strangely enough, one of the few things that sociologists of various persuasions seem to agree about *in general* is the 'importance' of education. It is quite interesting and instructive that Everett, writing in the famous first edition of the *Encyclopaedia of the Social Sciences* in 1937, should say that 'Education is perhaps the most useful tool of social control but it works for militarists and class conscious snobs as well as for humanitarians and men of vision' (Everett, 1937: 347). In the process of social control, defined in the wider sense of any influence exerted by society upon the individual, whether conscious or unconscious, she described education as potentially *more useful* than families or firms or other groups. In a world of rapid technical and economic changes which had led to the widespread breakdown of 'individualist assumptions', education is seen as the one public experience through which all must pass. In a world much given to 'economists, engineers and technicians', Everett would have delivered education largely into the hands of 'prophets, poets and artists', in the hope of combating what she saw as the growingly wrong balance between individuals and society. Modern education was inevitably massively organized and incursing, and was important enough to need careful watching.

Few sociologists would disagree with this sentiment, despite the fact that they are notoriously quarrelsome people in terms of their views of how man in society works. Indeed we shall not be able to do very much by way of analysing their claims about education until we understand a little about what it is they focus their disagreements upon in general. Although we shall see in detail as we go along how different types of social theorists develop their cases, we can assume from the start that:

(1) different social theories involve differing basic ideas or assumptions about what is 'really real';

(2) man is endowed with mind and consciousness, he experiences the world, himself and others subjectively *as well as* objectively;

(3) men conduct their activities in pursuit of ends, goals or purpose through actions which are habituated and rule-bound. This is not to say that they do not experience feel-

14

ings of freedom or personal uniqueness. The age-old debate about free-will and determinism attends to a perfectly real aspect of the human condition. The problems which it raises cannot be 'solved' and certainly not by sociologists. Their task can only begin, indeed, when the assumption is made that man's will and his conception of it are the products of his social time;

(4) in more modest terms, men share values and rules, some of which become deeply embedded in consciousness, others of which remain more superficially active, all in manifold contexts of power;

(5) how and why and to what extent this sharing takes place in the everyday life of a society, and what it means for activities like philosophizing about or socially analysing that life, are the very problems with which we are concerned. It is right that this should sound thoroughly circular, for that is how we shall assume that social process *is*.

Men in society are created by and recreate objective events and relationships which they experience as individuals subjectively and inter-subjectively (between themselves). Those variously viewed and experienced events and relationships which carry obvious personal reality also have more to them than just 'how they appear' to particular men.

It is around the balance between 'appearances' and what 'lies behind' them, that philosophical and social theoretical battle has raged. We cannot avoid the warfare in seeking to understand *social control*, for it is exactly about man's activity or passivity, his exact status as control*er* or control*ed*, or both, that conflict has centred. Some social theoretical views place the origins of the social and of consciousness in some potent single force, initially outside of man, for instance, in material circumstances, as with Marxism. In this sort of view, men can appear to be very much the product of forces and relations beyond their control and hidden from them until they manage to grasp the words and concepts that puncture appearances and give an access to reality that may then be 'worked with'. Others view social events as existing in their own right,

15

independent of human wills, and exerting a coercive influence upon them, there ready to be analysed by scientific methods as to their cause and functions, in the spirit that Durkheim advocated. Yet others place prime emphasis on the dominance of consciousness and language, very often raising major problems as to the entrapped nature of social knowledge itself. For instance, anthropologists like Winch (1958) believe that the rule-following aspect of social life is so exclusively important that no one except fully-imbibed culture members can 'get on its inside'. Once on its inside, the problem then is of getting back out, of being able to treat a form of cultural experience as a 'topic' when in fact we possess it as a 'resource'. Indeed there may be a questioning of whether there is any sense at all in which we can talk of understanding or explaining a 'form of life', social or intellectual, other than in its own terms. Sociologists who believe that the world *is* talk and associated symbolization, requiring constant reaffirmation and repair from its participant members, are called ethnomethodologists. They are a specific sub-type of a congerie of believers who are drawn towards the 'man is free' pole, loosely called phenomenologists.

Positivism

In recent years, many of the differences between these views have been polarized as a debate about 'positivism' and its place, if any, in sociology. Very crudely, positivists are described as having a belief in an 'out there' version of reality, which the scientist taps as he moves from hunch via test to truth (laws, etc.) in a given paradigm (a shared way of seeing, working and judging in an intellectual area). Valid objects of knowledge are held to be given to experience, whether they be natural, like rocks and rivers; or social, like values or interaction. Because of this 'positivist sociologies necessarily tend to reduce the social to given observables, to behaviour, interaction, etc. and to measurable and controllable reports of experience, attitudes, statements of value, etc. on the part of human subjects' (Hirst, 1975: 179). What has usually been argued to be wrong with doing social science in this way is that it entails a notion of men 'made' by and passively responding to forces 'out there' and beyond them. Positivistic sociology, it is said, does not allow for the fact that man has subjectivity and is capable of reflexion, that is, has free will and imputes meaning. Phenomenologists would say that it 'reifies' (makes misplacedly concrete) the social. Man is 'different' in this respect and his subjectivity may only be 'grasped' or entered into via empathetic understanding. There has been a specific rejection one by the other of those who believe that natural science methods can be applied to the social, and others who believe that only humanistic 'understanding' is possible. This difference, traditionally represented as being about method, is shot through with other considerations. Traditional positivists and subjectivists in sociology are *both* empiricists in that both accept the givenness of objects to experience, differing rather as to which objects are given. When phenomenologists are faced with the fact that men experience the social (rules, habits, customs, laws, expectations, etc.) *as* perfectly concrete, they tend to reply anti-positivistically that the *sociologist* ought not to, or else he cannot investigate such experiences as phenomena worthy of explanation. Sociologists, then, have special problems of participating in their 'data' which are potentially overcomable.

All this needs to be distinguished from essentialist views of knowledge as well as from shallow and partial manipulations of ideas about the relationship between knowledge and power. On the latter score, positivists are charged that their accounts, by sustaining an atmosphere of tested, expert knowledge, shore up controlling forces and groups in a society who may turn such knowledge into exploitative social technology. Functionalists, for example, who treat all societies as having the same problems, tasks or prerequisites, and who analyse social activities in terms of which problems they help to 'solve', are regarded as especially dangerous on this score. They emphasize the self-correcting (equilibrating) forces within societies which operate to combat 'breakdown' and argue that getting social members to share norms and values is a key element in this process. What seems to be overlooked is that it is the *a priori* and unexaminable element of their theories which leads to difficulties, not its positivism. Marxists, who would accuse positivists of driving a wedge between the necessary unity of theory and practice, solve these traditional problems by abolishing them in favour of one penetration of reality by one form of belief which has escaped the ideological disability of all others. No wonder that most Marxists, in a way quite different from functionalists (because their beliefs are essentialist and require the test of revelation rather than revelation via test) also place great importance for explaining social reality on shared values or ideologies. In post-revolutionary societies, adherents to communist social theory accord vital emphasis to correct shared belief. Marxists view capitalist societies as essentially conflict-ridden and prone to dissolution, because groups called 'classes' experience fundamentally differing interests generated by their relations to productive processes and their ownership. Owners expropriate 'surplus value' and control society's 'super-structure', which includes all forms of knowledge and belief, in their own interests. Correct grasping of Marx's delineation of this state of affairs constitutes the beginning of knowledge of the way out.

'Order' and 'control'

Questions of how human 'meaning' is generated and shared (or imposed) lie at the bottom of most well-known attempts to plot out differences between sociological approaches. Dawe (1970), for instance, distinguishes between approaches where the primary emphasis is upon *order* or *control*. Order approaches emphasize external constraint upon men (they are 'ordered'); control approaches dwell upon society as the creation of its members (they 'control' their meanings and relationships) – 'one views action as the derivative of system, whilst the other views system as the derivative of action' (p. 214). Dawe argues that these two approaches are doctrines, proposing utopias or *im*possible societies out of the clash of which modern sociology has been forged. Many sociologists have acted as if Dawe had *shown* that actual societies were, or could be, 'action' or 'control' *places*. The air of crusade has been increased by distinctions like that of Wilson's (1971) between 'normative' and 'interpretive' paradigms in sociology, giving the impression that 'shared values' or 'freedom' are real social choice-points. In fact, men's 'freedom' socially does not spring from the absence of control but depends both quantitatively and qualitatively upon both those controls built into and those exerted around him for its type. The bridges between us, along which our understanding 'grasp' of others flows, are made up of shared, collective meanings, individually experienced.

Culture – the accumulated experience, meanings, rule-systems, and forms of understanding of groups and societies – is the stuff out of which human biology is transformed into social individuality. The development of social self in its relationships to other persons and objects (called *socialization*) is a complex and continuous process. The combination of our 'take' from experience with individual biology produces *self*, uniquely conscious, imbued with identity and capable of activity. Such a social individual is, in terms described by Mead (upon which we will expand later), capable of controlled feeling and reflective intelligence in a way not possible in the non-human organism. Such a self stands in dialectical (i.e. reciprocal) relationship with its own impulses and the external world. Uniqueness is built in alongside physiology and culture, and all this is clearly 'different' about human experience and makes its explanation more complex. But it certainly does not rule it out from objective scrutiny as *just* subjective and end-directed (teleological).

Understanding and explanation

Explaining other people's behaviour is not the same as understanding it from their point of view. How I come to be writing this book is explicable in terms of the laws of biology and physics, my motives and intentions (not to mention personality, need-dispositions, etc.), the politics and economics of university departments (experienced as the requirements of

19

job and role), the operations of formal and informal networks of academic publishing, and so on, and so on. Getting to write a book, as with getting to post a letter, getting married, lost, or educated involves complex sets of activities, carried on by individuals within a culture which are at one and the same time massively patterned and repeated, while uniquely experienced and individually malleable. The empathetic grasping by another of the meaning to me of writing this book is also perfectly possible. If I call this 'understanding', following Jarvie's (1972) terminology, we can distinguish understanding my subjective state from understanding an explanation of my activity (or anything else for that matter). Explanations might be made of my activity, even by someone who had grasped my subjective intent, that might have been unknown to me or unacceptable in my judgement. They might even be beyond my grasp unless I learned (and was in a position to do so) the language within which they were couched. We might want to argue that certain sorts of sociological explanation ought to contain (or refer to, in some form) the facts of my subjective state, but it would be difficult to argue that all explanations properly called sociological should.

Indeed, no great sociological approach is *just* subjectiv*ist* (where only the contents of consciousness are given meaning) or wholly objectiv*ist* (where consciousness is explained away entirely in terms of 'something else'). We do tend, though, to see sociological progress as one polarized position swallowing up another. Perhaps this is because social reality is so complex, because social theory has moral relevance (and moral positions in their nature tend to be pre-emptive), and because 'knowledge communities' experience human struggles where who *knows* best and who *is* best get mixed up. We need to constantly remind ourselves that all an approach like Marxism, or interactionism, or functionalism or ethnomethodology can do is to strike a more or less complex balance about the priority of the individual or society, involving a consideration of biological-species-personality factors, economic-material influences and normative-value-cultural realities. It is possible to plump for one type or level of explanation as basic and to see the rest as derivative (or epiphenomenal). But society's (and sociology's!) existence depends upon there being reciprocal relationships between these levels. No known form of social theorizing has yet satisfactorily (i.e. without raising more problems than it has solved) swallowed up all others. Of course there can be no 'final proof' for it, only the test of asking what one loses at the same time as enjoying the gains afforded by using a particular approach. My argument is that to understand the manifold nature of social control, we must understand the manifold nature of the social, shown up sufficiently only if we consciously juxtapose major theoretical approaches.

2

Social control
and models
of man

Differences between sociological approaches are concerned with the very nature of individual/person and social group/ relationships. Views of social control span the entire spectrum. At the one extreme, some sociologists would want not to use the term at all, as it presupposes a reified view of the social which, being no more than the product of men, is infinitely revisable by them. In old fashioned terms, this represents the full flowering of the belief that if you don't talk about something it will go away, whereas if you do, it will come to pass. It is perfectly consistent if one believes, as some sociologists do, that the world *is* talk. At the other extreme would lie a view of man as essentially the same mentally, governed by universal master patterns, everywhere. Differences in culture would be merely superficial, accidentally or randomly generated or borrowed, covering up fundamental identities in structure. Both of these views, while graspable, are absurd.

A kit for all seasons

A basic, usable conceptual kit for viewing social control which could be tested generally against experience would consist of no more than

(a) a model of an actor whose self is 'made' out of the action of experience of culture upon biology
(b) within whom develops the capability to act reflectively upon his intelligence and environment
(c) as a result of the cumulative and qualitatively transforming nature of the experience of social formation.

Influences upon him would change from initial childhood to old age, some being more crucial than others. In all societies, the acquisition of language is highly important in self-formation. In some, first mass, first job, first marriage, first degree might be more or less salient. The activity of becoming social *is* the activity of becoming *ac*culturated, which always includes some means of acting back upon the culture which forms and controls. The culture in its turn is a product of and is part of the economic, familial, class, religious, political and other aspects of society. *Social* control merges comprehensively with self and interpersonal control, cultural, political and other forms. And *control* exists end-on with influence facilitation, coercion, self-impulsion and so on. Their explanation is far from being the province of only the sociologist. The psychologist, economist, political theorist as well as the poet all have their corners, and the fullest available explanations would require their conscious mutual awareness.

If we think initially about the issues involved as openly as this, then we will be in a better position to penetrate the vocabularies used in the work at which we look. We shall see, if we look at various conceptions of it over time that 'social control as a specific topic for sociology seems to be less popular now than in the past, when it was closely related to a concept of the source of deviance as being essentially located in the individual. But as the source of deviance has come to be located in the contradictions of the social system, the idea of

controlling deviant individuals has become somewhat re-
pugnant, and social reform itself has begun to look more than
a little naive to a sociology penetrated with the knowledge
that deliberate change always has unanticipated consequences'
(Pitts, 1968: 394). We shall argue that distaste for the term
notwithstanding, social control is not a disposable process.

The origins of the term

If we go back to the origins of the term, we find them very
much embedded in the wider social as well as the intellectual
problems of their time. 'Much of the impetus ... comes from
sociological adaptation of the Darwinian tradition.' Its emergence 'indicated a waning of the utilitarian concept of the
natural harmony of self-interests' (Pitts, 381–2). It took place
at roughly the same time in European and American sociology,
though the term as a turn of phrase was essentially American,
coined by E. A. Ross in 1901. Ross drew his ideas from
several sources, though Martindale (1961: 321) sees the
French sociologist Tarde's influence showing clearly in his
conception of society as 'a kind of fiction ... people affecting
one another in various ways' and of a collective mind growing
out of interactions over generations 'evincing itself in living
ideals, conventions, dogmas, institutions, and religious sentiments which are more or less happily adapted to the task of
safeguarding the collective welfare from the ravages of egoism'
(Ross, 1901: 293, quoted in Martindale). In society so conceived, social control referred 'to the manner in which the
interests of the individual and those of society are combined
and ordered'. Societies differed and hence so did the nature of
social control. What Ross called 'natural society' and natural
order appeared 'when basic human impulses are able to work
themselves out without interference' (Martindale: 322).
Natural order derived 'from the spontaneous meshing of
men's personalities with their inherent capacities for sympathy
and sociability, on the one hand, and from their sense of
justice and capacity for resentment on the other' (Pitts: 382).
Ross saw the societies formed in the American West during

the gold-rush as approximating such a 'freely competitive society'. Persons came from various backgrounds to work out 'a society on the basis of differential abilities and a foundation of natural dependability, trust and fairness' (Martindale: 322).

Such societies were distinguished from 'class based societies' of opposite type, where 'we no longer have social control in the true sense but *class control ... the exercise of power by a parasitic class in its own interest*' (Ross: 256). Between these two extremes, the 'ordinary' possibilities of social control were displayed, involved with group interests, and growing in importance where a given group was ascendant, tightly knit, self-conscious or tending towards selfishness. As intended and function-fulfilling dominance it included public opinion, law, belief systems, education, custom, religion, personal ideas (such as basic gender definitions), personality, social evaluation and ethical systems particularly in relation to survival and elites. Ross believed that rational action should take non-rational elements into account in creating a moral order to replace that threatened by growing population density and heterogeneity, in which the elimination of moral idiots by natural selection could no longer be guaranteed.

Ross's ideas raise all sorts of problems for us today about the relation of terms like 'function' and 'intended' and they constitute what now appears as a weird mixture of conservatism and liberality. But we can draw two points of lasting interest from them: firstly, that the means of social control are various, spanning the basic forms of social identity transmitted in childhood (like sex-typing), through to law; and secondly, that their importance will vary depending upon the type of society.

Ubiquity and variety of type was also the hallmark of Durkheim's conception of the 'collective consciousness', elaborated at around the same time as Ross wrote about social control. Durkheim's own definition of the *conscience collective* or *commune* was as 'the set of beliefs and sentiments common to the average members of a single society [which] forms a determinate system that has its own life' (Lukes, 1973: 4, quoting Durkheim, 1933: 79). It could only be realized through individuals, but pre- and post-dated them.

25

In the English sense, it connoted both 'conscience' and 'consciousness', in a way which goes right to the heart of individual/social relationships – 'that these two form a single concept in French means for all French sociologists, that internalized sanctions are amalgamated, at least to some extent, with awareness of social milieu' (Bohannan, 1960: 78). The collective consciousness strongly marked societies in a state of *mechanical solidarity*, where parts bore strong resemblance one to another and had an enveloping 'cell-like', segmental quality. Religion pervaded everything and law was characteristically repressive. Through increases in 'moral' and 'dynamic density', mechanical gave way to *organic solidarity* in society. The strong and pervasive collective consciousness itself gave way to *collective representations*, socially generated, referring to the group's 'mode of thinking, conceiving and perceiving and to that which is thought, conceived or perceived' (Lukes: 7). Such a society had a much more advanced division of labour, much more individuality, rational morality and so on. Education, in such a society was, for Durkheim, especially important in dealing with questions raised by the ethic of individuality and the division of labour's demands. Individuals are still 'constrained' by the *collective representations* of laws, customs, religion, language and so on. They are 'socialized' into them, follow some of them as necessary means-ends procedures, fear others as sanctions and so on. Durkheim's constant insistence was that these 'social and cultural factors influence, indeed largely constitute individuals' (Lukes: 13). People have frequently found Durkheim's model confusing and metaphysical. He certainly believed that nothing preceded the social, that some types of society were simpler than others and that there was a 'double givenness' of individuals and society. There was a constant problem of there being both a sufficiency of the collective consciousness built into individuals and of its attention to their needs. There was a constant and somewhat fearful 'play' between the society and the individual within whom we could say certain elements of the collective consciousness become deeply *constitutive* of personality, while others remain merely *regulative* of our behaviour.

Models of men

It is clear that from the start the notion of 'social control' and similar contemporary ideas, pointed to forms, mechanisms and processes in differing societies whereby

(1) society 'gets into' the individual to form social personality capable of 'acting back', as well as
(2) the cultural, economic and social structures of the societies themselves within which these processes take place.

Anthropologists have long recognized that there are complex but determinate links between culture and personality. Marxist social theory has always argued that consciousness is a product of material conditions. Types of human identity, thought forms and language structure are always generated within and influenced by particular politico-economic and cultural mixes. We cannot divorce views about society from those about the men who inhabit them, but we can try to clarify the linkages a step at a time.

Every social theory certainly contains an explicit or implicit model of man, as well as of society and interaction. Now there is a sense in which we should *expect* a social theory's man-model to be its weakest or least developed point. After all, sociologists are not specialists in terms of man's physiology, psychic life, moral attributes and so on, all entailed in a 'rounded' model. And indeed, many old social theories – or present ones in their original versions – developed in eras when philosophical debates or psychological knowledge were different, sometimes cruder. They correspondingly 'worked' with much simpler models than we would be satisfied with today.

Marxian man

Marx's model of man, for instance in his early work (elaborated roughly before the mid-1840s, which some Marxists want now firmly to reject), is essentially a *philosophical* one, initially without much psychological or social flesh. It is, nevertheless, quite a warm and appealing creature. Man is said to have a *species-being*, whose true nature resides in its ability to create, to produce, to work. This nature is thwarted by the conditions of capitalist production (just as it was in earlier societies), which take the fruits of his labour away from him. Production not only does not belong to him, it is directed against him. He becomes *alienated*, therefore, not only from the object and process of production but from his own *species life*, himself and his fellow men. He is prey to the degradation and false-consciousness imposed by the propertied classes, who themselves in their turn fail to avoid the same alienative fate, though they enjoy it the more comfortably.

Later on his work and certainly by the time of his writing the *Grundrisse*, the 'notebooks' preceding *Das Kapital*, Marx was delineating a less general and philosophical 'human nature'. A more concrete, though equally exploited, creature staggers under the burden of the huge weight of his labour 'objectified in capital' opposing him. This man was still one who had given up his fundamental activity of control, now to be securely entrapped by the 'fetishism' of commodities and the advancing technology of modern industry.

We do not need to enter into the debate about who nowadays has a monopoly over understanding the 'real' or 'relevant' Marx to see that the most important aspect of his 'man' is that he is inconceivable without activity, and except in relationship, creation, making, work or production as his fundamental activity. His 'state' in a given society depends directly upon his position *vis-à-vis* the forces and relations of production, the latter being the real, economic foundation upon which the political, legal and other superstructures with their own forms of social consciousness are erected. Various forms of domination flow from them. Given an awareness, called 'dialectical', of the unity of subjective and objective factors – history is made by men pursuing their ends not just as they please but in circumstances given to them – the Marxist mass awakened to its own unstoppable power may escape certain forms of social control via revolutionary activity. There is no 'psychology' or detailing of a socialization process in Marx, for reality in no important sense lies within the individual. But we should not assume, as some vulgar folk do, that this automatically debars meaningfulness of the individual.

Durkheimian man

What has been frequently represented as the 'alternative' or very differing model to that of Marx's emerging from the nineteenth century, is the creature represented by Durkheim. To a large extent, his man is equally general and philosophical and lacking in psychology. Durkheim was as all against the *reduction* of social phenomena to individual psychologies and the value of introspection as an analytical tool as he was against a view of society as some sort of embodiment of human will or purpose. However, there is no paradox between this and the view that he finally came to through the study of primitive religion (1968, first published 1915), that 'society exists exclusively within the minds of individuals'. Parsons in fact believes 'that Durkheim must be accorded, with Freud, the credit for what undoubtedly is the most fundamental of all *psychological* discoveries, namely that of the fact of the internalization of culture as part of the personality itself, not simply as providing an "environment" within which the personality or the organism function' (1956: 19).

Durkheim's man was born biological, with instincts, but beyond that – 'The child, on entering life, brings to it only his nature as an individual.' Heredity transmitted instincts and a very simple capability for animal social life – but was 'not sufficient to transmit the aptitudes that social life presupposes of man, aptitudes too complex to be able "to take the form of organic predispositions"' (Fauconnet, 1956: 29). Each new generation of plastic, newborn infants requires a long and cumulative period of interaction, experience and exposure to become a truly human being: 'Man is man, in fact, only because he lives in society.'

Durkheim's detailed account of the socialization (he never used the term) process now sounds to us rather sonorous and old-fashioned. He talks in terms of the spirit of egoism in the child having to be tempered with altruism. The child must be inducted into the fundamental elements of the morality of his time (it is vital to note that 'moral' here derives from 'mores' –

social custom and usage, etc. – rather than connoting 'ethical'. For Durkheim society *is* a 'moral force'). In early twentieth-century France, these were the spirits of discipline, abnegation and autonomy. These could not and ought not, for the good of society, be combined in the same degree in every individual: 'society can only survive if there exists among its members a sufficient degree of homogeneity ... the essential similarities that collective life demands. But on the other hand, without a certain diversity all cooperation would be impossible' (Durkheim, 1956: 70). In modern society, to the danger of building too much or too little or an inappropriate selection from society into the individual, there was added the danger of the division of labour itself becoming anomic or pathological. Education is assigned a vital part in the task of achieving some part of these vital balances whose longer term resolutions might have to lie in a more thoroughgoing revival of associational life, involving a combination of bureaucratic centralization and individual atomization looking rather like the medieval guilds.

Never the same again

Both Marx and Durkheim in their differing ways set out to destroy the credibility of utilitarian man. This rational calculator of pain and pleasure at the margin, this joiner and leaver at will, had long borne much of the burden of social mythology. He might be conceived of as nobly savage, spoiled only by contaminative social process, or as essentially selfish and capable of surmounting fear and despond only through the surrender of a portion of his interests to the mutual protection of the larger social whole. Neither Marx nor Durkheim could accept either of these versions or their visions of optional or pre-sociality. Modern society for both of them had certainly brought man to a point of crisis. For Marx this was epitomized by the imminent collapse of the material forces of capitalism, forces which were inevitable and unstoppable but capable of being mastered by those who had penetrated their essence. For Durkheim, the division of labour at large threatened to become overwhelmingly anomic or deregulated. Complexly differing social niches simply could not be filled adequately by a population among which the spirit of individualism became extended into class-based politics. Social control for both was a many-layered phenomenon, the reality of which lay deep in the mainsprings of a society's fundamental nature, at the base, in the rules behind rules, and nearer the surface in particular formations of personality, institutions and practices.

While we shall explore these aspects of their ideas more fully below (Ch. 5), we can note here that they and others shattered for our time any viable notion of simple man, simply controlled. They shared with others the experience of having to cope with, and give sense to, the tremendous nineteenth-century growth in both knowledge (particularly that which was science-based) and economic productive capacity. Certainly by the end of the century the contrast had never stood wider between Darwinian necessity and human possibility dissipated in exploitation. The temptation to seek a return to less complex modes of existence was one to which ultimately both Marx and Durkheim succumbed. But we know, and they may have guessed, that they had been prime agents in declaring that journey to be beyond possibility.

Much of what has happened in terms of twentieth-century social theory and the men which it posits, consists in elaborations and denials of these themes. With other streams joining the confluence they provided in the first two or three decades of this century a most marvellous upwelling of ideas about the relationships between the individual, society and knowledge. Freud's vision of man's powerful but hardly controllable unconscious provided strong ground for the further break-up of rationalists assumptions. The growth of behaviouristic man models in psychology associated with the work of Pavlov, Watson and others provided even more, but obviously from very differing sources. Meanwhile, developments in Gestalt psychology tended to pull the other way. Even more, a gentler version of social behaviourism foreshadowed in the American work of Thomas and Cooley and developed by Mead showed that reflex and reason and the social were not the fused enemies of freedom. At about the same time as Mannheim, in the tradition of Marx, was depicting man-in-a-class for whom truth floundered in ideology, whose ideas stood as disguise for his 'real' situation and interests, Mead and his students elaborated the notion of truth residing in the successful adjustive act. It was becoming increasingly clearly worked out that man could be variously placed in relation to the importance of social process and knowledge, both in social psychological terms and in the emerging sociology of knowledge.

Meadian man

Mead develops an 'in-between' notion of the social individual, less mechanical than Mannheim's man and more selective than Cooley's 'looking-glass self'. 'Mead's formulations point towards a model of man whose chief characteristic is precisely the ability self-consciously to reconstruct a universe better suited to his own needs' (Farberman, 1973: 266). Man self-consciously mobilizes response to 'thereness' in the universe, which he 'picks out'. He has unique perspective but has to adjust his tested perceptions in order to live communally. Mind and self emerge in a social matrix out of joint acts. Self-conscious response depends upon communication via significant shared symbols. Neither mind nor self precedes social process, but that process plays upon biologic self to produce the 'me' – 'those incorporated responses of other, to the beginning of one's own acts' – and 'I' – 'those responses of ours which come over against the implanted reactions of others to our own initial phases of action. Where the "me" is the organization of attitudes of others which we incorporate, the "I" is our response to the attitude of others' (p. 270). Self arises from I–Me dialogue in individuals, taking, evaluating and revising action.

The bridge between the self and the act is the attitude (or incipient act): 'an inner mobilization of energy which is preparatory to an external act' (p. 268). This mobilization is selective relative to the individual's purposes. It is sometimes observable as gesture, e.g. fist-clenching prior to attack, and as such assists in the anticipation of response. Sequence and direction (where is the interaction going?) are essential to this: 'to the extent an actor is able to imagine the future goals and consequences of his action, his present route of decision need not be taken blindly' (p. 269). Communication also pre-

32

supposes this, 'for only when an actor can respond to himself as others respond to him, can social life continue'. The dynamics of symbolization make this possible: A and B share capacity for response, including response to their own responses. Language is crucial to this 'for it enables us to hear what we are saying and as such allows us the possibility of responding to ourselves with the same kind of response to which others may react' (p. 269). We can deliberately mobilize and anticipate it. Perspectives can be jointly evoked. Mind emerges, in effect, from role-taking. Reflexiveness enables the individual 'to incorporate through each social act the conditions of society'. Inner dialogue carries this on so that 'a unification of perspective or common point of view can be arrived at even while the attitudes of expected responses of others are held only in imagination' (p. 270).

Whole networks of rules and roles are internalized, as well as the attitudes of single others, as the 'generalized other' or social organization. But for Mead interaction always has a creative tendency, springing from altered response and hence newly-established relation. As Farberman pungently puts it, Meadian man's *dictum* would stand as 'to exist or to be is to know that one is in interaction'.

Mead's social behaviourism contains a philosophy offering the chance of reconciling widely opposing traditional poles or problems, whose potential has yet to be exploited. Miller argues that Mead's position affords a genuine way round some of the ancient problems of the relationship between man and knowledge. He presents Mead's central idea as being that all 'meanings and structures, of which we are conscious, and all universals, which are means by which we think, are created by mind in conjunction with a world that is there' (1973: 4). He proposes that this view is much nearer than the notion of 'knowing as apprehending what is the case' to what recent social science has suggested is the function of mind: to give 'new characters to objects in the process of the adjustment of the organism to its environment and the environment to it' (p. 5). It neither entails man seeking quiescience, for novelty is constantly emerging in process, nor a relativism in the sense of every man his own truth – 'minds are a part of nature; and

33

the individual is in the perspective, not the perspective in him. Minds cannot exist apart from perspectives any more than perspectives consciously created exist apart from the mind. Minds emerge in individuals only insofar as the individual can enter into the perspective of the other, and such perspective is by definition objective' (p. 21). All hypotheses emanate from individuals but require truth status by public test. 'In its broadest sense, to share perspectives is to share attitudes, and the attitudes of the community, in their widest meaning, are summarized in terms of the categories with reference to which the experiences of members of the community are interpreted. This may be stated in terms of the attitudes of the generalized other' (p. 34).

Interactionist man

Mead's teaching (for his works were not finally collected until well after his death) created disciples and a diffuse set of sociological movements, peopled by a number of similar types of men whom we can call symbolic interactionists. A great deal of their work on social process and identity has focussed upon 'problem' and deviant areas of experience, no doubt partly because of their intrinsic interest practically and theoretically, but also because of ease of access to the study of the politically and legally less powerful. The bearing of this work upon questions of social control is often poignant and direct.

As exemplified in Becker's sociology, for instance, inter-actionist man is rational, learns and shares group perspectives, chooses while he undergoes process (Becker, 1973; Becker *et al.*, 1968). Goffman's man lives in a darker less controllable world of impression-management and institutional force (1959, 1961). Matza's, even when publically labelled thoroughly deviant is 'proud' in the sense of being in and somewhat still 'of' straight society as well as simply entitled to freedom from our opprobrium (1964, 1969). No doubt many of the dif-ferences in their man-models reflect variations in the identities and careers of these interactionists-as-researchers. It would be of a piece with their credo if this were so.

While it is characteristic of these sociologists to lack an articulated picture of social power, for their theory and methodology points them directly at 'local' group and individual levels, they have called to arms in terms of values and bias (or power) in sociology. Becker has asked 'whose side are we on?' in the study of us–them society and on grounds of expedience *and* morality chooses the underdog (1967). Matza has insisted upon 'naturalism' in research, a complete faithfulness to the perspectives of the subjects of study in order to overcome our traditional 'correctional' tendency when viewing deviance.

What sociologists such as these have brought powerfully to attention is the strength of social ascription via labelling. Sticks and stones may break my bones but names will always hurt me. Through the words of the criminal delinquent, the hobo, prostitute, drug-taker and so on, in a tradition going back particularly to Chicago in the 1920–30s, interactionist sociology has shown, through detailed observational study, how the 'outsider' is social creation. Durkheim suggested that society 'needs' and naturally produces its deviants who 'function' to revive and strengthen collective sentiment. In this sense, deviance-creation is part of society's large-scale 'control' mechanisms. Becker's classic view *in extremis* promulgated the view that deviant behaviour is simply behaviour successfully so labelled, and is not definable in terms of an inherent quality of the activity. This suggestion had the tremendous power both of moral shock and proper sociological scepticism. Of course such a view can all too easily be pushed into friendly bathos for all wrong doers, in a way which Becker himself would not license (Becker, 1973; Taylor *et al.*, 1973). But we owe to such interactionist work the solid achievements of the distinction between primary and secondary deviance: the demonstration that while many are called to initial acts of deviance, few go on to deviant careers via repetition, public labelling and inner-self-confirmation (Hirschi and Selvin, 1967); and evidence that delinquents experience neutralization and loosening of moral bind only in limited experiential areas (Matza, 1964).

None of it however requires us to give up the belief that individuals and groups in a given culture know only too well the link between good-bad, deviant and non-deviant. That this shifts over time, and that groups may differ significantly over particular items of belief and behaviour is true. But it is equally true that the means of deviance bestowal and enforcement in certain public sectors is massively known and clearly links with political and legal agencies, (legislature, courts, legal profession, police, etc.) as well as conceptions of right, duty, justice and morality. These are not glibly reducible to the exigencies of power structures.

Indeed our experience of deviance-normality bestowal is part of the very fabric of everyday life. Garfinkel (1956) shows how we constantly tend to relabel in the light of new information about people, how we 'remake' biography to render it consonant with moral facts about an individual, like first-known acts of deviance. The pressure is towards the non-dissonant comfort of 'he always must have been like that'. This view is of massive importance for schooling, whose task *is* the production of normality (with concomitant generation and identification of deviations therefrom) in any society, as that normality is currently defined (Davies, 1973a). We shall see below that there has been a great deal of work on labelling children and upon the creation of pupil identity and career types in our schools which is central to their control aspect.

Parsonian man

In pursuing Meadian man on to his present day interactionist sons (and we shall come back in a minute to their phenomeno-logical cousins), we have shot past the type who was without question dominant post-war socio-man. He has very much been the changing creature of Parsons's social theories and he was of explicitly mixed parentage. He was composed mainly out of aspects of Durkheim and bits of Weber, with a few gestures in the direction of Pareto and grew up in the 1930s and '40s, maturing in the '50s. He was entitled 'action' man, to connote that this was his essential social business. As 'ego', he lived in interaction with 'alters' within shared orientation systems. Endowed with Durkheimian plasticity, his early up-bringing was rather Freudian, within the increasingly intense and unstable nuclear family. The formation of the key aspects of his personality system hinged around the exigencies of the oral and oedipal phases, negotiation of which produced him available for elementary school at six, distinguished only by internalized sex-typing and independence level.

Within the personality system, the dark pressures of Id were harnessed to the cultural appropriateness of the need–dispositions network. The organism-personality participated in the social and cultural systems, the social system being concerned with the integration of acting units in the form of personalities engaged in roles. Role performances were always patterned in terms of finite choices as to the pursuit of one's own or others' ends, emphasis on performance or status, affective enjoyment or neutrality and seeking limited task performance or more general relationship (he called these the 'pattern variables'). In Parsons's own words, 'the major functional problem concerning the social system's relation to the personality system involves learning, developing and maintaining throughout the life cycle adequate motivation for participating in socially valued and controlled patterns of action. Reciprocally a society must also adequately satisfy or reward its members through such patterns of action if it is to continually draw upon their performances for its functioning as a system. This relationship constitutes "socialization", the whole complex of processes by which persons become members of the societal community and maintain that status' (Parsons, 1966: 12). The cultural system, at the same time, legitimated the society's normative order, defining members' rights and prohibitions and who might use power.

While societies evolve and differentiate (particularly in terms of their cultural and social system relations), their operations are always analysable in terms of four functional categories or prerequisites: *adaptation* to the environment (the specialism of the physical organism), *goal attainment* (the specialism of personality systems), *integration* (attended to by the social system's patterns of personalities in roles), and *pattern maintenance* – 'the maintenance of the highest "governing" or controlling patterns of the system' (the special domain of the cultural system) (ibid., p. 7). Rather like a Chinese box, these specialist systems can be thought of as having to solve these four problems within themselves, too, as would institutions and organizations within them, e.g. families, schools, churches, governments, etc. For instance, a school as part of the educational system would operate to create and modify motivated personalities which, as role types, it also served to differentiate and allocate towards different forms of adult position. It would play a part through the creation and display of social and cognitive scenes in society's integrative and pattern-maintaining areas. Each school would also experience internal adaptation, goal attainment, integrative and pattern-maintenance problems, as would each of its sub-parts specializing in one or more of these, as well as its individual actors *qua* personalities manning the roles.

'Over'- and 'faulty'-socialization

As Parsons has changed his wordy and formal terminology more than once over time, this brief account of his man is deliberately composite and must stand for dominant post-war American (for which read the whole sociological world) functionalism in which he was only one, though the dominating, figure (compare Davis, 1966; or Johnson, 1961, in their accounts of 'man' and socialization). The chief complaint about functionalist man has long been that he was 'over-socialized', too highly and neatly inducted into a normative system by powerful agencies of socialization – family, peer-group, school, neighbourhood and job – operating in consensual harmony where conflict had been cybernized away (or sometimes, the accusation went, put out of mind like the ghetto) (Wrong, 1961; Dahrendorf, 1958). Parsons and others have often been written about as if they never conceived of man living in class-, interest-, conflict-based society, experiencing sentience and doubt. This view, fashionable and self-sustaining as it has long been among sociologists of differing persuasion, is as silly and dangerous as anything that functional sociology has ever produced.

Parsons's schema may be overly formal, pretentious, wordy and inherently conservative, but they also pick out vital aspects of man and society. Men in some degree *are* socially formed, consensus in society *does* derive from widely shared values, social process *is* end-directed and partially self-monitoring and so on. It makes perfectly good sense to ask of a social activity 'what is it for?' as well as 'why is it like that?'. Indeed, insofar as we are conscious, prefigured and choosing beings 'what's it for?' questions will always *be part of* 'why is it like that?' ones. What we need to ensure is that, when we ask such questions, we expect the answer to come back in terms of a world where power and ignorance are unequally distributed and rather more explicitly self-sustaining than is the case in much recent functionalism. 'What's it for?' as sociologists from Marx to Becker have in some degree reminded us, depends upon whose point of view one is asking the question from. To say 'society's' is not to answer but to pose a further question.

The second sort of major criticism that has often been levelled at functionalist man models is that they have to rely on a concept of 'deviance through faulty socialization' to account for malfunctioning and change in social systems. Or it has been said that deviance has to be viewed as a product of 'under' or insufficient socialization into appropriate norms. Our discussion of interactionist man points to all sorts of problems with this. 'Undersocialization' (not knowing how to go on?) raises logical and technical problems: 'faulty' socialization, moral and political problems (in whose terms?). We have already seen what Matza (and others, like Cicourel and Sudnow) suggest that deviants are *multiply* socialized into straight *and* other worlds. They have the choice, and the location in the social structure, which does not require any further explanation in terms of predisposition to account for why they deviate. Any residual mystery is quickly dispelled by grasping that enforcement agencies, despite efforts to the contrary, inevitably display bias that runs along (perhaps even essentializes) 'respectable lines'.

All this is a bit of a minefield, particularly when we approach the limit of the debate which says that all rules (legal, aesthetic, social, cultural, moral, intellectual) exist only and always to protect and enhance the interests of existing power-holders (whether their basis is economic or otherwise), *vis-à-vis* the lower class, proletarian, black, uneducated, etc. .... That rules entail enforcers–enforcees, adjudication, etc. goes without saying. Equally generally, it seems possible that their basis in consent and coercion will vary, and that the altruistmutualist-exploitative content of different rules will be dissimilar. The unwitting deviant (and he may be *entailed* in a good model of the 'first offence') may be said with some justice to be inappropriately or under-socialized (for he cannot know some aspects of what he is likely to pluck down upon his head), or to be drawing upon mischosen or experimental bits of his repertoire. On the other hand, the recidivist *may* be the most completely socialized of all. The deviant neophyte cannot quite be fitted into a 'free choosing' model, not least because he cannot choose the experience of sanctions which have not yet descended upon him. In that sense, his repertoire is 'deficient'; but that is the 'boo-word' to end them all in modern education debate.

Parsons's account of deviance is both characteristic and interesting: its motivation lies in past learning, personality or the present situation. Frustration of role expectations leads to 'ambivalence' directed either at alter or the entire normative pattern. Failure to discharge it is likely to lead to compulsive conformity *or* alienation (though they may be shot through one with the other – illness being the 'prototype of passive alienated behaviour'). Universalistic and achievement oriented society, which characteristically forces deviants into groups together, gives it much leeway. In respect of radical and dissenting 'deviants' their ambivalence as claimants to be true defenders of the main value pattern is always the social control bridge back, via 'selling out' (would Parsons recognize the 'moral holiday' aspect of the contacts kept by non-radical, non-dissenters with utopian views?). Society's institutions for preventing the desire to deviate from building up, e.g. family, peer groups, art and entertainment, religion, the saloon or socialism, do not work perfectly, so 'secondary institutions' control its legitimate forms, e.g. gambling. It is of course this sort of lumping together, the regarding as somehow 'functionally equivalent', that sets Parsons up the nose of those whose institutions he unseemly likens. We can certainly take Goldmann's point (1968) that when a term like 'deviance' gets applied to areas like radical politics, or consensus-challenging social beliefs (like, say, an activist Marxism in western politics) then the rhetoric of the social system has jumped tracks into politics and philosophy to threaten control via trivialization.

Schutzian man

While the new ideas of the interactionists doing work on deviance contributed a great deal to questioning the adequacy of functionalist man and the 'correctional' perspective, the man who inherits the non-judgemental earth most completely is Schutz's wide-awake, vivid-present person and his phenomenological heirs. Combining the actors of Weber and Husserl (see Gorman, 1975), he exists in a physical, social and cultural environment with a biography and a unique 'stock of knowledge in hand' (the accumulation of his previous experiences). He has projects, purposes or plans – interrelated sets of things which he wants to do now or later, among which he has to choose according to his interests. The world around him takes on more or less 'relevance' (in 'zones') in the light of the purposes which he is pursuing. 'The world at first appears as an infinite series of open possibilities. Our unique biographical situations, the numerous paths in life meaningfully experienced only by individual travellers, limit these to a series of possibilities relevant to our subjective interests, what Schutz calls our "problematic possibilities". We decide which of these problematic possibilities and their corresponding projects to adopt, considering them one at a time. Each successive consideration corresponds to a succeeding temporal state of consciousness, indicating that while we decide what to do we are simultaneously growing older and constantly adding experience to our mental baggage. We are never the "same" persons in considering each of our problematic possibilities' (Gorman, 1975: 2).

Viewed as a free and subjective actor, Schutz's man begins the pursuit of his projects with his in-order-to motives (all inter-connected to his life's project). Having so done, he then mobilizes because-motives (past-based motives for doing things), and the typifications of the world stored in his stock of knowledge. Past experience tells him that under similar circumstances, he can do things again and that others reciprocate this knowledge and his motives. These 'others' range as types from 'consociates' with whom we have close and informal we-relationships, to 'contemporaries', predecessors and successors, with whom we have more or less anonymous relations.

The freedom of Schutz's man in the common-sense world is not, however, necessarily put to very dignified place. Man habitually restricts himself in behaviour in terms of the 'socially correct', quickly-applied recipe, acting with automatism and half-consciousness. However, Schutz also asserts that he *can* transcend the common-sense world by breaking with the habitual, routine and impersonal. This freedom is not expanded upon, but we can take it to be an *existential* one, a necessity from the point of view of constructing meanings in situations at hand. Schutzian man emerges as a complex and rather irresolute mix. His freedom is posited as inalienable yet he appears capable of allowing it to fall into desuetude. He allows the world of his own creation to become misplacedly concrete and to dominate him. Yet what he puts up, he can take down. He could put aside his daily draught of role playing, essence of bad faith, in favour of the cup of existential freedom (Douglas, 1971).

Schutz pointed out that there are inevitably very special problems about the study of these free men. He advocated that the sociologist should 'homunculize' or turn them into puppets pursuing idealized action types. Only thus could their world making and creative possibilities be captured second-hand (or order) by the constructs of the social scientist. His work – along with the 'loosening' deviancy studies, a revived interest in the sociology of knowledge, and (history may reveal as significant) social protest events in the sixties – was one of the positive influences upon the origin of ethnomethodology.

Ethnomethodological man

The term was invented in a Wichita jury room to cover the case of practical reasoning revealed under those special circumstances by Garfinkel (1968). Both he and Cicourel, the other major figure associated with the origins of this style of work, had a background of work in the organizational process, deviance-labelling area. Cicourel's early well-known studies had to do with 'normal performance' definition in a High School (with Kitsuse, 1963) and selective enforcement practices by police agents (1968).

Their work along with that of their associates makes the claim to unhinge virtually all traditional sociology, as confusing 'topic' with 'resource'. The claim is that traditional sociologists have used societal membership as the means of 'understanding' the meaning of social action painstakingly measured by 'objective' device, but never in such a way as to manage to include the essential ingredient of *true* social explanation, the intent and meaning of the actor. Hence Durkheim is exploded for not reading the notes left by the suicide-intent, and positivists generally for clutching at objectivist explanation when intuitive grasping (difficult enough) is all there is. As we noted in Ch. 1, the possible counter-attack to this is that it involves a confusion of understanding (of human freedom, uniqueness, meaning, etc.) of action with explanation of that action. The extreme point of the counter opposition might be a *structuralist* belief such as that of Levi-Strauss (see Leach, 1970), arguing on the basis of a universal human mental capacity or characteristics that cultural phenomena simply consist of complex, penetrable variants on basic exchange systems.

The ethnomethodologist would disclaim that his work was 'for' anything in the sense of making objective findings about the world. Giglioli puts it very clearly: 'Ethnomethodologists suggest that, in contrast to Durkheim's dictum (or to certain positivistic interpretations of it), social realities are not a "fact", but an ongoing accomplishment, the often precarious result of the routine activities and tacit understandings of social actors. In this perspective, speech acquires a particular importance. It is essentially through speech that men communicate with their fellow men. Yet speech becomes understandable only in connection with social interaction. This embeddedness of speech in interactive process makes social meaning "reflexive" and "indexical". In other words, in natural conversations sentences are almost always incomplete or ambiguous. Language provides a variety of different labels to refer to an object or action; moreover, the social meaning of a term shifts with the situation' (1972: 13). But the man of ethnomethodology, the speaker-bearer, sharing common-sense knowledge with others, gets by pretty well. The interpretive procedures *whereby* he gets by are the proper concern of ethnomethodologists.

They will research these by total immersion in the collection of data about speech and other communicative acts from very limited interactive scenes. During the very detailed analysis, the researcher will aim to keep his own 'rules' scrupulously apart from those of his subjects: 'he must relinquish the point of view of the ordinary member concerning his existential nature of the bureaucratic organization, for instance. He must instead study how members talk about and "do" bureaucracy, in this way revealing *the way in which* bureaucracy is real – as opposed to taking that reality for granted and instead studying "its" (presumed) relationships with other such "structural elements" ' (Roche, 1973: 323). He must take the traditional 'looking behind' function of the sociologist to one of its logical conclusions, by becoming highly organized 'judgemental dope'. Of those parts of social reality whereby his subjects do not speak, he must be silent.

Cicourel has in several places given us hints as to how ethnomethodological man acquires social structure as a child. His ideas in general draw their strength from Chomsky's linguistic concepts of competence and performance and surface and deep structure. Cicourel is unhappy about the conventional use of *role* in 'normal' sociology as well as the loose way in which language is assigned a place in child development. He is interested in using ideas in generative grammar to explain how children acquire 'interpretive procedures', which 'as opposed to surface rules (norms) are similar but in many ways different to Chomsky's distinction between deep structure (for rendering a semantic interpretation of sentences) and surface structure (for designating phonetic interpretation to sentences), for interpretive procedures are constitutive of the members' sense of social structure or organization' (Cicourel, 1971: 139). Norms and attitudes are no more inherently meaningful than semantic interpretations. Values and normal forms in a culture depend upon the prior acquisition of interpretive procedures, indeed in an initial or simplified form they must precede or accompany the acquisition of grammar: 'just as a child is capable of producing grammatically correct utterances that he has never heard before and is capable of understanding utterances that have never been heard before' so 'actors are capable of imitation and *innovation* with little or no prior rehearsal' (1970: 28).

The very emergence of interpretive or basic rules 'must allow for the operation of memory and selection procedures that are consistent with pattern recognition or construction, active ... and passive ... hypothesis testing, and be congruent with the actor's ability to recognize and generate novel and "identical" or "similar" behavioural displays ... Basic or interpretive rules provide the actor with a developmentally changing sense of social structure and enable him to assign meaning and relevance to an environment of objects ... Normative or surface rules enable the actor to link his view of the world to that of others in concerted social action and to presume that consensus or shared agreement governs interaction' (1970: 28-9). Basic rules and normative order are always in interaction, as are surface and deep structures in linguistics. Basic rules provide actors with a common scheme of interpretation, enable actors 'to articulate general normative rules with immediate interaction scenes' and govern the sequencing of interaction (1970: 41). They are invariant properties of everyday practical reasoning, acquired by the child along with language, in childlike ways, giving way to adult forms with aging. Norms and rules are not 'given' instantly acquirable features of social structure: 'whatever is built into the members as part of their normal socialization is activated by social scenes, but there is no automatic programming ... children continually rehearse their acquisition of social structure (and language) in ways reminiscent of actors rehearsing a play or translating a written play into a live production' (1971: 153). And despite lack of empirical evidence, we must plausibly assume acquisition of initial interpretive procedures prefacing language use.

Though, then, the mechanisms are still unclear and we still

wait for many examples of basic rules or interpretive procedures, Cicourel underlines the importance of understanding 'how adults routinely expose children to the normative order' (1971: 168). The tenor of his argument adds weight to the reality and autonomy of the child-world. Just as the young child should be viewed as speaking an esoteric language fluently, not merely producing an incomplete or inadequate adult language, so his 'conception of the social world should not be studied by imposing as-yet-unclarified adult conceptions of normal social structures'. We know little about the child's developmental problems in rules acquisition but should assume that childhood conceptions of social structure are real and the basis from which change works.

Tom, the teacher and Chicken Little

It is this sort of orientation that has led to the mood summed up by Dreitzel when he says that 'children are not simply *tabula rasa* which mysteriously responds to the input of stimuli by adults, and adults are not simply stable factors in the child's social environment, but are themselves prone to change under the impact of their offspring's challenge' (1973: 6). He couples this with the view that society under 'corporate capitalism' produces a social climate in which the 'misery of the nuclear family and the prevailing injustice of the school system' plus 'the ever more intensive exploitation of labour' claims many victims, among whom 'children may be the most deplorable group' (ibid., p. 9). They are trapped in the nuclear family, failing 'because the retreat from a deteriorated public sphere into a Sartrean hell of the emotionally overburdened seclusion of privacy provides for a pathogenic socialization milieu' (ibid., p. 12). And the school is just as much trouble!

The hysterical tinge to such rhetoric should not conceal the chance that the 'conception of children as essentially deficient vis-à-vis adults has, in practice, led to no research into children *qua* children' (Mackay, 1973: 28). Traditionally, socialization has been 'glossed', as opposed to 'explicated' as *interaction* between adults and children. Basing his ideas on Cicourel's conceptions discussed above, Mackay wants to argue that children are not only competent interpreters of the world, but are also 'in possession of their own culture or succession of cultures'. Despite the limited evidence for this, if true 'the study of adult child interaction (formerly socialization) becomes the study of cultural assimilation ...' (ibid., p. 31). Rendering it problematic requires us to orient to children and adults (including teachers) as cultural strangers.

Mackay presumes that cultures are of equal worth, strength and power, so that when he offers a lengthy transcripted example concerning Tom, the teacher and Chicken Little, where teacher keeps on referring Tom to the 'facts' of the story, he sees a 'paradox' in that 'the teacher relies on the child's interpretive competencies to understand the lesson but treats him throughout as incompetent (i.e. she creates or gives the "correct" answers). The child is treated as deficient ...' (ibid., p. 39). Mackay is here dissipating, in a way which has become tediously familiar, an important point in a thoroughly muddled view of truth, knowledge, correctness, etc., by deploying a degree of analytic sleight of hand. Firstly, Mackay does *not* make clear his tacit assumption about the equal worth, correctness, etc. of cultures. Secondly, the use of terms like 'incompetent' and 'deficient', though having heuristic value, also has strong moral loading. And thirdly, as with a great deal of 'neutral' ethnomethodological reporting which simply does conversational analysis, the whole 'meaning' of the conversation is built up without reference to the actors' consciously recounted intentions. We are asked to take it that what teacher and child were 'on about' is readable just from a transcript. This is a curious sort of behaviourism in methodology. What *are* the teacher and child really on about? While teachers no doubt frequently demotivate children by too rapid procedure to 'the case', it is our case here that the world would indeed be an 'alternative' one if teachers abrogated the belief that in certain respects they know more and better than children. Ethnomethodological man (or child) is the constant conscious receiver or transmitter of messages. His image is hand-tooled to the presumption that everyone knows best (because no one knows better). This can be a tremendously powerful unhinger of our taken-for-granted assumptions or preconceptions both as sociologists and laymen. But put to use it brings us only exotic travellers' tales – whether from class, jury or poolrooms – unless we can connect it to other ideas which show us that man's world is frequently structured so that he may only just be able to see the end of his nose. And children are *not* self-sufficient spontaneous generators of all that they need to know, though teachers' structured situations frequently lead them to disastrously contrary orientations.

Homo eclecticus: a suitably complex character?

We have expended this much space in looking at 'models of men' in order to clarify what sort of a creature it is that is being socially controlled (or not) by education or any other relevant bit of society. There is really a double bind from our point of view. All the work which we can draw upon *about* education contains assumptions about man (often tacit), while the worth of any work which we try to use depends upon what sort of aspect of man we have at the sharp end of the application. Men live in material conditions in the main no more or less of their making than the social reality which surrounds them. At a very general level, social systems do seem to exhibit similar problems, though of course social existence is always in process and the particular contents and qualities of that process are what matter to us as live our lives. Men play in, at, with, for and despite their roles. The links between social freedom and necessity may be illuminated – that is, validly and in part explained – by a large variety of social theories but not exhausted by any one of them. Parsons's, Mead's, Durkheim's, Marx's and Cicourel's children may all go to the same school but they take to it, experience within it, and bring away from it quite different things, as we shall see. I will have missed my point if I have not effectively suggested that real children and the actual adults who teach them, contain *all* of the elements which differing sociologists blow up and claim to be dominant.

3

The rise of
mass education
1: Britain

More determined than determining

Much of what goes on in schools and other education-specialist
establishments also goes on elsewhere. A great deal of formal
and informal learning takes place in the family, among peers,
in religious and leisure organizations and so on. Vast amounts
of instruction and training are given 'on the job' – perhaps
more than occurs specifically in school (Clark, 1964). It would
be quite fruitless to try to evaluate whether school was 'more'
or 'less' important than other agencies of socialization and
cultural transmission in our sort of society. Sociologically, we
are better equipped to answer much more modest questions
like 'important for whom, and in what particular respect?'

Present day ordinary-language philosophers of education
tell us that the pursuit of any conception of the worthwhile
may count as 'education' so long as certain procedural grounds,
like indoctrination-avoidance and emphasis on intrinsicality
are respected. They translate the worthwhile as 'the acquisition of certain fundamental forms of ... public modes of

experience, understanding and knowledge' (Hirst & Peters, 1970: 60), of which 'some seven areas can be distinguished, each of which necessarily involves the use of concepts of a particular kind and distinctive type of test for its objective claims'. Questions of how these might be effectively transmitted and the import of successfully so doing, are all referred to the social scientist.

He would do well to begin his analysis by conceding a 'philosopher's point'. Education is not merely socialization, except on a hopelessly extended view of that concept. But neither is it, as practice, necessarily predominantly 'about' acquisition of currently conceived fundamental forms of knowledge. Schools also transmit – and not as some rather suspect and contingent part of their task – beliefs, values and evaluations which have to do with broad aspects of social structural relationships. Pupils 'learn' in school a significant portion of what they know about their own 'worth', their relation to others and to the political, economic and stratificational systems. They gather this from the explicit messages of the curricular content presented to them and the manner of its presentation and evaluation, as well as from the more general 'noise' surrounding these communications. Pupils are treated as well as taught by adults who may be highly conscious of a great deal of their activity, but who also are themselves shaped by history (including their own biography) and structure (including that of the school itself) and who *cannot* know what pressures play out via them in total.

The education system has a complex, historically evolved position in relation to other aspects of social structure and process. It is, as often as not, talked about as being determin*ed by* rather than being determinat*ive of* these structures and processes. Technically, of course, the relationship must in some degree be reciprocal. But *if* educational experience is largely an induction into the worthwhile and the normal, however currently defined, we would indeed expect it to be leaned upon and to take the impression of outside forces. An acceptable sociological evaluation of these forces and education's autonomy or subservience in their respect must be historical.

Britain, or little by little: complexity outlined

Behind the Acts, lies ...

Historians, like sociologists, disagree of course over what constitutes a proper evaluation of evidence. The really obvious markers of the past 150 years of British development look to be the great central decisions of government: the initial support from public funds of the virtually exclusively dominant church influence beginning in 1833; Forster's Act of 1870 creating the public elementary school; Balfour's Act of 1902 which gave the English grammar school its modern footing; Fisher's Act in 1918 whose intention to move towards 'secondary education for all' was checked by economic difficulty throughout the inter-war period; Butler's Act of 1944 which actualized the modern structure of stages (primary, secondary and higher) and laid down the credo of treatment 'according to age, aptitude and ability'. But while these are the obvious markers in respect of public education, we know that behind them private provision (which still accounts for over ten per cent of all places) reformed – indeed in the nineteenth century perhaps this *had* to precede any mass extension of secondary schooling – and the 'religious question' transformed. The basic accommodation of state schools to religious instructions was set with the Cowper–Temple clause in 1870. It was to be the only compulsory curricular element, accompanied by the right to withdrawal of their children exercisable by parents. That same spirit is enshrined in the present 1944 provision, though of course the actual provision of Church schooling, whether Anglican or Catholic (other denominations and faiths ever having provided only very small numbers of places) has declined steadily under the twin masters of increasing costs and growing secularization. Many parents, teachers and church authorities would, no doubt with some justice, extol the virtues and authenticity of a proper 'religious' schooling though they could not point with any certainty to its effectiveness even in conserving the flock. In sociological terms, at the risk of some crudity, we can regard church provision (like Welsh-language provision), particularly at the secondary level, as being deeply implicated both with parents' wishes for an 'orderly' experience for their children and the continuing complexities of 'selective' placement. Evidence as to the resistance of the church voluntary-aided or controlled grammar schools as well as their 'selective moderns' in the face of local authorities' comprehensive reorganization plans, frequently attests to the way in which prestige resists parity and pleads faith and cash shortage while so doing.

On top of all this, there goes the much less centrally directed growth of the higher educational system, particularly at the university level. Ancient Oxbridge (never forgetting the Scottish universities) was joined by utilitarian London in 1832 and then a flood of redbrick in later century, with a long gap until the 'new' wave of the 1950s and '60s. We shall say very little about higher education in this book, but it is absolutely vital to grasp that the universities have in a quite crucial way set the market price to be respected by secondary schools for entry to themselves and their cousins – historically teacher-training and the upper levels of technical college work, and more recently the colleges of technology and the polytechnics. The specialism of secondary education and historical conceptions of 'normal' good achievement at higher education entry are inexplicable except in respect of the autonomous, gatekeeping (and personnel production) functions of the universities. The derivations (or reverberations) have long dominated a whole system having at its centre the 'desirability' of subject – mastering certification.

We finance, you consent?

Perhaps most important of all, so far as the school system is concerned, key changes have often had to wait upon changes in (or deficiencies of) local authority structure. The British system is one of central legislation and part-finance, with a national inspectorate of historically dwindling importance, coupled with local authority autonomy. In education as elsewhere, local authority obligations are often laid down in general and 'open' terms, with real gap between minimum required and maximum permissible performance. The real heart of educational control has long been finance and advice as manipulated from the centre. Over time the Board, Ministry, then Department Circular has often been mightier than the Act of Parliament. Forster meant little without the attendance compulsion introduced later, the curricular possibilities enshrined in the Board of Education Regulations, and the associated means of paying central grants without which local rates could not have provided adequately. It was via the famous Cockerton Judgement, of 1899, precipitated by the operations of the School Board *auditor* in London (with the less than shadowy figure of Robert Morant, Secretary to the Board of Education, in the background), that local authorities' spontaneous attempts to bend their elementary provision to provide 'secondary' places for bright children was stopped. The Balfour Act which followed it, 'giving' the grammar schools and the obligation to provide for them to the County Council, meant very little until the Regulations of 1904 and 1907 clarified the distinction between the 'higher elementary' and grammar school tradition. The latter took its down-to-the-present 'arts-science' split curriculum from the associated grant conditions. 1944 really belongs to Hadow and Lord Eustace Percy – a Report and a bureaucrat conjoining to provide a wider ladder for children of differing types. Tripartism (grammar, technical, secondary modern school distinctions) is not enshrined in that Act but in the Ministry Circular which followed, pointing out that LEAs could fulfil their 3Rs obligation efficiently by such provision. Circular 10/65 which created the tempo necessary for moving towards mass comprehensive provision, while exhorting authorities to prepare reorganization plans, had its 'teeth' in the Department of Education and Science's statutory control over building plans and their finance – no building allowed which was not intended for or was palpably modifiable into 'comprehensive' provision. In 1975 the OECD investigators pointed to the continuing vital influence of powerful, closed bureaucratic planning forces within the DES (*Times Higher Ed. Supp.*, 1975). They did not complain about their quality or any lack of farsightedness, but rather of their normal operation in an atmosphere of concealment. The system of Central Advisory Council Reports –

Early Leaving, Crowther, Newsom, Robbins, Plowden and so on – with their 'appointed', consensual basis has played a vital role in providing expert validation for mundane changes (or their avoidance) in provision and practice. The unique British institution of the Schools Council, significantly the mutant child of concern about 'examining' beyond the 'conventional ability range', is an interesting expression of a system at once highly 'local' on an authority and individual school basis, but also highly 'central' via the traditions of examination boards, subjects and texts. Young's (1972) curiously muddled analysis, for instance, seems to fail to grasp that 'democratic' teacher control of the Schools Council might produce just the curricular output that has characterized it to date, or to consider that in a roundabout way it *is* a mildly *avant-gard*ish demand–response organization.

Leaving aside the further complexities of Irish, Scottish and Welsh regionality, there is nothing easy, then, about the growth of the machinery and control of British education. That it has always had a deeply political character goes without saying. Further it can be roughly 'matched' to economic developmental stages, with lag more obvious than lead: the broad consumer/literacy base, the development of elite skills, the broadening of mass skills and the moving into 'consumption' for all rather than 'investment' in the few, can all be sketched in (or prospected), as for other societies. In what senses has it effected social control?

Gentling our masters

1870 and all that

Any real fear of political revolution had passed in Britain long before the 1870 Education Act. In this respect, 1848 was a much more significant watershed, marked by the collapse of Chartism as a political movement. As historians like Simon and Wardle have pointed out, there were in effect substantial sorts of agreement between early nineteenth-century working-class leaders and radicals who, in diagnosing exploitation firmly believed that knowledge was the key to power (Wardle,

1974: 95). Advocates of 'moral force' like Lovett were far more characteristic than those of the physical kind in the class-war, and campaigns for cheap and freely available information (especially on politics), and working-class adult education initiatives were far from insignificant in the first half of the century.

Though figures for this period are not notoriously reliable, over 600,000 endowed and unendowed places for children in 1786 had swollen to 1·4 million day and 1·2 Sunday school places by 1833. A large measure of universal literacy had been achieved before 1870, when universalism was introduced out of a mixture of instrumental, altruist and fearful motives. 'Education as innoculation' had worked against the dreaded Jacobinism, persuading common men 'of the folly and inefficiency of turbulence'. Now the elementary Board schools which 'filled the gaps' left by church and private provision were intended by Parliament as utilitarian and rudimentarily social welfare in function, providing via drill methods for the inculcation of social discipline. 'Many schools, especially those in urban areas, had to face a flood of new pupils who, apart from being very reluctant scholars, were at a stage of sheer barbarism which the modern English teacher never experiences. Inevitably these schools had to set for themselves low levels of aspiration ...' (Wardle, 1974: 97), but given the immensity of their problem, their success was remarkable.

Simon argues that despite the languishing of the broadly based agitation for educational advance after Chartism's downfall, it was not possible by this period to impose a closed and divided class system of schools. Although it 'had not been originally envisaged that the worker's education should be so extended, least of all that control of schools should be handed over to elected bodies and the teaching of religion made optional ... events had forced the pace and mass working-class pressure contributed to ensuring that at least the first foundations of a universal system were laid – that education was no longer a charity but a right' (Simon, 1960: 35). Given the renewal of the grammar and public schools already well under way, 1870 *did* threaten to institutionalize class education, and church and middle class interests *were* notably successful in keeping radical and workers' interests off school Boards where they attempted entry. The class supply of leadership to industry and empire via the public and grammar school had, though, to be filtered increasingly through the merit-definition of examination success. The distribution and allocation of power and opportunity achieved by the late nineteenth-century system was 'a response to industrial and imperial demands ... made on a hierarchial class basis', but it is not self-evident 'that the Boards of Education, the government of the day, or individuals like Forster were motivated in some Machiavellian manner' (Little *et al.*, 1973: 9).

Elementary procedures, extraordinary results

Shipman sees the schools of this period operating in a context of the need for forms of social control to change as response to *modernization*, when 'secondary agencies' of socialization increase in salience, work changes in nature and meaning, and schools are required to prepare the population for the demands of organizations and the broader horizons entailed in possibly altered life-styles. He sees 1850 in England as a crucial watershed. Impelled by economic and technological change 'the phase of uprooting and disturbance' gave way to new patterns of culture and social organization. The 'silent social revolution', partly initiated by education, 'was also the product of better housing, better health, better social administration, more rational laws and a more adequate environment for family life' (Shipman, 1971: 158), while other forces made the distribution of political power more equitable.

By the turn of the century, schools were looked to positively to come to the aid of flagging Christianity and failing national physique as well as the generation gap and foreign competition. Education was debilitated by none of our doubts about 'deprivation' or 'compensation'. British schools were set to save society from itself though, as Wardle observes, the selected and non-selected were not notably expected to experience this in co-presence. Inspection of late nineteenth-century curricular patterns for elementary and higher elementary grades, in contrast to those of grammar and public schools, leaves no doubt that intended functions were of social control as well as economic placement. The normalcy of inculcating the child with the values of self-discipline, respect and humour drop as readily from the Elementary Code of 1904 as play and self-direction do from Plowden (and as no doubt with similar rhetorical depth). The elementary school *had* though settled and broadened in the eighties and nineties. Curriculum had been allowed, via modified financing systems, to diversify beyond the 3Rs for more than a fringe. The 'Codes', alongside a national inspectorate and the Board's highly influential *Handbook of Advice*, created a position *de facto* where central pressure short of direction as to the minutiae of content of curriculism under state finance, was a reality. White's (1975) account of Eustace Percy's work to abolish the Regulations in 1926, preferring as he did to trust the innate conservatism of the profession, inspectorial and teaching, rather than risk a Labour Government using their manipulation for 'ideological' ends, is a recently revealed and fascinating chapter to put against the cherished British belief that it is only beyond Calais that these damn dangerous practices have occurred.

Shipman remarks that in the restless, possibly near-revolutionary days following the First World War, authority fully appreciated the role of the schools: 'Teaching children to arrive punctually and regularly, to sit still for long periods and to listen to the teacher, to carry out instructions quietly and quickly and to endure these constraints without complaint, was a suitable preparation for working in the large-scale organizations of a mature economy and to live in the urban society in which private property was unequally distributed and in which the amount of public property was rapidly increasing' (pp. 161-2).

Whether that same authority recognized it or not, schooling never had the power to prevent the emergence of class consciousness. Its origin lay firmly back in the nineteenth century's shift in the size of work places, the changed nature of supervision and the boring nature of work. These were areas where there was initially much to be said on both sides of the factory floor, but where for long 'employers met workers head on in almost complete mutual incomprehension' (Wardle: 93). The effect was corrosive.

There's no chances like class chances

The pool forms

There is nothing particularly paradoxical in seeing the beginnings of state education in Britain as having much to do with basic economic pressures for extended literacy – the failure of technical education until well into this century is clear – *and* extended 'social discipline'. Much of what would have been transacted in late nineteenth-century schoolrooms would now, by any standard of discipline and educational ascription, be harrowing. But once created, and given changing demographic conditions, the system provided channels for the mobility-aspiring. Indeed, while technical education never really arrived until after the *Second* World War, before the First, the 'demand for general education preparatory to vocational training on the job ... was of great consequence to the expansion of formal education at all levels – elementary, secondary and higher – and at all levels the requirements were essentially the same' (Wardle: 64). These requirements were the provision of appropriate academic competence, the development of general intelligence and attitudes efficient and adaptable to employment. As the latter varied widely, so too would suitable, especially secondary, education. This, for Wardle, explains divided schooling and the explicit importance of the 'hidden curriculum'. Professionalism, too – 'one of the great Victorian inventions' (p. 65) – gave real impetus to secondary and higher education's growth. Medicine, army and civil service all took on modern form and strove to overcome nepotism and, with conscious democratic impulse, to widen the pool of selection.

Perception of changing occupational structures led to increasing numbers of parents attempting to assign their children to 'the pool'. As Bernbaum (1967) points out, clerical and professional occupations expanded rapidly and education took on new significance for a minority in respect of occupational, and hence social, mobility. In 1907, grammar schools were required to open 25 per cent of their places free to children from public elementary schools, providing powerfully increased impetus towards their attractiveness to the *petit bourgeoisie* for their children and a real pressure upon the quality of their curriculum. Glass describes the interplay of economic, resource and social factors on early twentieth-century secondary provision (and the Fisher Act never really managed an advance on them) as ensuring that 'the provision of scholarships did not catch up with the demand for them' (1961: 398). The operation of IQ testing and the 'social class image of the secondary school and its purpose', entailed that while working class children *could* secure their free places, 'working class parents who wished their sons to go to grammar school had to accept the fact that they would move out of their parental "class". Some parents did accept this fact – indeed they positively wished it. But many did not' (ibid., p. 400).

But mixed bathing takes time

Marshall aptly sums up the outcome of such pressures, particularly in relation to Free and Special Places. 'It may look at first sight as if the bourgeoisie had, as usual, filched what should have gone to the workers.' He is not surprised – 'the Welfare State is not the dictatorship of the proletariat and is not pledged to liquidate the bourgeoisie' (1961: 156–7). Middle class children fared better for a variety of material and cultural reasons under pre-1944 policy that was far from 'collectivist'. Banks (1955) shows with some clarity that fear of a middle class fall was ever more powerful than a hope of working class rise in respect of the competition for scarce places and pressure for modifying the non-grammar school provision towards qualificatory and 'selective' ends. Pressure from Trade Unions and Labour Party from the 1890s and 1918 respectively for equal opportunity and secondary education for all *was* real. But it was far more likely Lord Eustace Percy's conviction 'that as a lift or stairway to the higher storeys of the social structure' (quoted by Glass: 402) secondary education was falling short, coupled with Hadow in 1926 taking the conventional wisdom rising like a tide in the veins of education about types of children, that led to the 'equal but different' tripartism of 1944. That perfected the replacement of 'the nineteenth-century social class homogeneity of the grammar school' by 'a homogeneity of measured intelligence, the upper 20 per cent on the IQ scale' (Glass: 402). Outside of the social *cachet* and snobbery of private education it also ensured that the prestige of schools depended in future more on the classes which they prepared for than upon the classes which they drew from.

No one really knew with any precision what effect provision-changes had brought about in class chances until the LSE mobility work was published in the early fifties. This revealed that working class children had at last achieved a clear majority of maintained and direct-grant grammar school places – estimates ranging from an official 64 per cent down to the upper 50s, depending upon the boundary definitions for manual/non-manual, employed/self-employed categories used. As Glass pointed out, commenting upon the 1947 Scottish Mental Survey, if tests were the basis of allocation and were grammar schools to cover the 'top' 23 per cent of the population, $60 \cdot 1$ per cent would be working class in origin. But if only the top $6 \cdot 3$ per cent were to be selected, then only $48 \cdot 6$ per cent of the children would be of working class backgrounds. Given the extreme variability existing in the provision of places from Kent to Merioneth, the first implication of this was obvious.

Test procedures were in fact often of the 'school attainment' variety, without any IQ component at all, or adding in IQ only as an element. Though the cultural implications of IQ tests were already being strongly queried by the early fifties – indeed despite what now seems to be some of the unsavoury geneticist and theological-statistical devotion which they inspired, they always were in some degree – it must also be clear that the testing movement entailed social progress. It provided irresistible evidence in favour of the lower orders the force of which, alas, petered out towards the 'bottom' end of the occupational scale. But the presumption was that talent was, if not randomly, very widely distributed *and locatable*. A head-for-head 'class share' of grammar school places in the early fifties would have given 70 per cent to the 'working class' (ignoring the existence of private schooling), and it was the children of unskilled workers who most lost out. The evidence of the early sixties (Little and Westergaard, 1964), was that insofar as authorities moved away from objective – including IQ – tests in selection, class-shares became less equitable in respect of 'selective' places. There is, therefore, strong presumptive evidence in the light of what we know of the socio-politics of secondary school transfer in favour of continued objective testing, assuming that 'superior' places will continue to be in short supply. Even in the context of the 'common school', it requires a revolution in teacher expectations to provide adequate surrogate for tests of brightness.

Which problem do we abolish?

Viewing the history of British education as the history of access and opportunity is unavoidable in terms of how it seemed to those involved in it as well as its social effects. There is a real sense in which the beneficence of traditional curricula, teaching methods and forms of evaluation in our schools were not seriously or widely questioned until quite recently. In recent years, the cry of crisis has come from all sorts of quarters.

Down with schooling

Orthodox Marxism has *not* notably provided a source of challenge – Simon, for instance, believes wholeheartedly in education and the inevitability of the foreseeable comprehensive future. Levitas (1974) reveals a similar general commitment plus a eulogistic feeling for soviet practice. Wardle's study, on the other hand, draws its force from the 'radicalism' of an otherwise a-historical 'deschooling' *genre*, and though of great interest, its conclusions are palpably contradictory. Setting out to examine from an historical point of view whether formal institutional education has outgrown its usefulness, his contention is that 'education' has been hampered and stultified by historically recent (the last hundred or so years) association with 'schooling'. With Illich and others he argues that compulsion (average school life in inspected elementaries went up from 2·55 years in 1870 to 7·50 in 1897, and few now escape the 5–16 net), long with us, has only recently really exploded in terms of lengthening secondary experience for all and higher education for many. Formal schooling's rise has been accompanied by the 'invention' of childhood, and the subsequent intermediate category of 'youth'. Commercial exploitation is 'without doubt one of the most potent factors in the establishment of youth as an independent age-group' (ibid., p. 42), and youth has recently inherited many of childhood's former problems in education and the media. However, Wardle offers no further differentiation in his analysis of youth market and culture, or their relations to family background, educational experience, community type or sex. His restless youth are more than somewhat massified in American-radical style.

Contrary to this superficial analysis, youthful experience in our society, though in certain respects its tasters may have more in common now than ever before (but doesn't *every* age-category?) and be more self-conscious of its presence, is still in vital respects differentiated *particularly* along the lines of educational success and failure, and concomitant occupational destiny. Systematic evidence on this and accompanying sex, class and locality factors has always been curiously lacking, barring Musgrove's (1964) limited but still quite vital work (where he also laid out an 'emergence of adolescence' thesis in late industrial revolution terms). We still have to scrub around the limited confines of official reports and empirical studies, mainly of streaming in secondary schools, for our information other than on 'deviant' youth. That the nature of youthful participation in their 'culture' or group-relations can vary from the encapsulating and protective through to the passing and superficial does not seem to occur to radical critics.

Wardle does caution, though, against the deschoolers' American emphasis on the conformity-dropout malaise. He suggests that the values and attributes which English schools 'attempt to propagate in their pupils very rarely, in spite of what the deschoolers tell us, reflect the received values of society. More often they are engaged in a conscious crusade against the dominant culture ...' (p. 108). Given this, he sees the child 'at the point of conflict between several more or less opposed cultures, his family, his peer group – and a clash here is very likely – the mass media, the school'. He is faced with taxing tension 'which can lead to productive questioning' or 'to a flight to authority, a refusal to think for oneself, and this indeed is one of the most conspicuous characteristics of youth culture'. Young people are faced less with 'exposure to over-whelming indoctrination than ... an embarrassment of choice' (p. 109). Nothing sounds less like a plea for deschooling, par-ticularly when coupled with clear historical evidence of children's growing non-reluctance to attend schools. Indeed Wardle explicitly rejects the deschoolers' plea for a return to *lassez-faire*, albeit technologized. Whatever less than lauda-tory features like imperialism and social Darwinism, lack of parental power (shallowly treated), and so on, that his re-searches reveal, Wardle concludes that education in schools has an 'apparently inescapable liberalizing effect', the evidence favouring the view 'that the effect of mass schooling upon society was that of an irritant rather than a soporific' (p. 151). At the same time he believes that 'the power of schooling to form personality is not so great as it has often been supposed to be both by the advocates and critics of institutional educa-tion'. I would agree with him on both counts. Moreover I feel that his 'agreement' with the deschoolers concerning the over-organization of youthful activity, the dangers of teaching as professional monopoly, growing uniformity of approach and a tendency to centralize decisions does not amount to a *prima facie* case, even where established in its particulars, for closing the gates.

Down with knowledge

The crisis has also been presented in recent years as one about the 'nature of knowledge'. Subjects or disciplines have been solemnly indicated not so much for contingent boredom in presentation but as carrying the seeds of 'expert', hence class, exploitation; for having 'status' because job-attached, hence 'denying' it to those exercising humbler talents and unfairly bestowing it on those preparing for the upper occupational reaches. Combined with the facts of occupational inheritance, the plea becomes one for the policy of institutionalizing the superiority of 'common sense' as something apparently naturally unsullied by the reified world of evidence or rational or conceptual test. Egalitarian though the thrust superficially is, and valuable in forcing the examination of preconceptions and practices as to curricular and 'ability' categories (Young, 1971), the view is a response to misunderstood historical forces within our system.

High expectations, low jobs – muddled solutions

The crisis which presents itself to some as one about the 'nature of knowledge' is, in fact, more nearly that of a system facing up in a serious way to how it inducts neglected groups of its clientele and then holds them within itself. That is to say, historical forces have brought us to the point of having to face up to the problem of mass *education* rather than training or control. The recent relative failure of some sectors of secondary school is quite spectacular, especially as indexed by truancy and disruption in respect of holding and willingly engaging certain age and ability segments of their population. (see Cave (ed.), 1976; Turner, 1974). We simply have not faced up to the consequences of a situation where high expectation of education by children, parents and teachers working their way out in schools embodying increasingly modern methods within, faces an occupational structure without, which is changing at snail's pace per school-generation. Mass desire for education has now given way to a mass access, but entrants are still in the main faced with a 'common curriculum' designed for an uncommon intake in the selective school. The post-war secondary modern school failed, *en masse*, to evolve distinctively non-grammar school curricular practice (Taylor, 1963). Their major mission from mid-fifties on was to squeeze maximum examinable talent from the top end of their streamed innards. We have yet to think through the shape and feel of the 'equality of access to knowledge' curriculum which I believe that Lawton rightly advocates (1975). We are in a muddle organizationally, too. The advocates of comprehensives long may in the main have wanted 'a policy of deliberate social mixing'. In practice local authorities have kept ability and not social class measures, though some, alarmingly, now keep neither, allowing 'neighbourhood' and 'parental choice' to settle secondary school child intakes. Both of these latter factors are virtual guarantees of continued secondary school hierarchy, though what may be entailed in setting them aside in the short run is a real accretion of bureaucratic power and direction within authorities. Many appear to run systems more than mildly crucified by stretching over these disparate points of principle. In their midst, individual schools struggle wittingly with grouping and curricular experimentation, while yet others chase the shadow. Teachers, parents and children can find themselves in situations of social, ability and knowledge mixing such as very few of them have previously experienced. Passions are excited which the system, except at the level of daily endurance, has hardly yet learned to understand let alone cope with successfully (Davies, 1976).

The new *noblesse oblige*

In this context, the cry of the common-sense curriculum (Young, 1975) and de-schooling (Illich, 1971; Reimer, 1971) are both peculiarly unlovely forms of handed-down, intellectual Ludditery. That the inhabitants of education's 'domesticated' establishments with guaranteed clientele and loosely applied tests of fitness (Carlson, 1964) need regular jolting, almost goes without saying, though the line between reflectiveness and narcissistic irritation is narrow. But the real sociological puzzle in respect of 'deschooling' is why the opinions of its protagonists have been taken so seriously. Their social analysis is almost entirely superficial. In Illich it rests upon the unexplicated belief in the desirability of retreat to a non-mass consumer based society (as opposed to a *better* one or analysis of whether a not-already-consumer based society should make the traverse). This is coupled with a rather naive and shadowy reliance upon the power of the computer and conviviality to provide knowledge as wanted. In the earlier work of Reimer, an honourable American academic-journalist fringe (see also Goodman, Holt, Kozol) does moral steam-raising in respect of the known defects of the public system. (see Postman and Weingarter, 1971, for its perfection of the explicit denial-rhetoric). Its effortless moralizing has the strengths and weaknesses of affording instant access to itself. Its major themes are altogether parasitic on a much more proper scholarship displayed by investigators like Henry and Jackson, to whom we shall turn below. As to Freire, often also ranked among the deschoolers, his claim must stand upon its 'humanistic Marxism', which we will also discuss later, though teachers of reading everywhere will no doubt be interested in his suitably de-rhetoricized claims.

No doubt some of the deschoolers' success has something to do with the appeal of their stridency to elements of the mass media (note, though, the possible explanations of Illich's relative shortness of shrift in relation to his attacks on medicine). It probably has more to do with the growing guilt, insufficiently slaked by the power of sound analysis, at the centre of the intellectual educational establishment. Direct inspection of historical shift and turn could provide part of the proper grasping of roots which this guilt requires. Every generation is required to rewrite its history but not to lose it. The wilful cutting adrift from historical reason by self-styled radicals believing that sound social analysis was born yesterday out of their discovery that education is a massive empire of interest groups doling out and receiving the possession of knowledge unequally, misses the point that having the knowledge is good, lacking it troublesome. They have it and would withhold it only from others, and in the name of populism. More precisely, in many cases they would have their late-arrived version universalized and others made subservient to it. Marxisms fall *par excellence* into this category and it is largely to their application to the analysis of Amerian education which we now turn.

4

The rise of
mass education
2: United States

Quite recently there has been an interesting growth of attention to the rise and functions of American public education which has gone under the heading of 'political economy'. It draws upon Marxist economics (and political attitudes) as in the work of Gintis; radical and orthodox traditions of work on underdevelopment, imperialism and planning, as in Bowles and Carnoy; and historiography, sometimes under Marxist-tinged impetus, ranging from the careful to the thoroughly polemic. We shall look first at some of the historical work. Before we start, bear in mind the State and district localism, and the lack of federal (central government) incursion which, until very recently, characterized the United States system. This means that good historical studies require limiting to particular times, issues and locations for their focus. The ones at which we look have this character but their authors are far from loath to use them as a platform for generalization.

'Critical history' goes to school

History as deinevitablizer

Katz, whose work we shall take first because it deals with an earlier period than the others, explicitly pronounces his ethic. It resides in declaring his interests in the present discontents of American education as a preface to careful analysis of its past. The past itself is interesting because its clear understanding can be liberating in respect of present inevitability. Historical structure must be examined to see 'how techniques become traditions' (1971: xix).

His view is that 'by about 1880, American education had acquired its fundamental structural characteristics', which have remained thoroughly resistant to what little attempt there has been to change them, because they serve the powerful interests of professional careers invested in the system, and benefit the children of the affluent disproportionately highly. The system is, 'basically ... universal, tax-supported, free, compulsory, bureaucratic, racist and class biased' (xviii), and all appear to be depressingly inevitable.

Its purpose for over a hundred years 'has been, basically the inculcation of attitudes that reflect dominant and industrial values; the structure has been bureaucracy. The result has been school systems that treat children as units to be processed into particular shapes dropped into slots roughly congruent with the status of their parents' (xviii). Despite present inevitability Katz argues that it is vital to grasp that in the early nineteenth century alternatives *were* posed. Bureaucracy only came to be thought inevitable as a combination of industrial growth and certain sorts of values conjoined to crystalize 'bourgeois social attributes'.

Boston public education

He exemplifies this in relation to the development of Bostonian public education after 1800. Here and elsewhere 'four major alternatives, four models of organization, conflicted in the first half of the nineteenth century ... paternalistic voluntarism, democratic localism, corporate voluntarism and incipient bureaucracy' (p. 5). Around them, debates as to size, control, professionalism and finance raged. Then as now, they were emotional and value-laden debates about society and proper standardization. Organizations, which 'derive their peculiar importance from their positions as mediators between social change and social structure' (p. 6), were at their heart. 'Paternalistic voluntarism' was the first to prosper, but it confounded 'public with pauper' (Katz seems genuinely surprised that in 1805 the upper classes' impulse was to save the lower orders from their inherent degradation without notable prior consultation). It gave way to 'democratic localism', an essentially rural growth difficult to transplant in towns where 'urban loss' denied it suitable soil, but handy as a solution to the problem of religious minorities (mainly Catholics in New York in the 1840s. 'Noble' (echoes of recent ethnic beauty claims?), it was also short-lived, giving way to single institution 'corporate voluntarism' in secondary and higher education ('a combination of public goal and private control, wrapped in the mantle of disinterested service' (p. 27) exercised by non-peculating trustees). In the main, this too had to give way to the *public* high schools of 'incipient bureaucracy' produced by men who attacked mid-century Massachusetts' democratic localism as either 51 per cent control or 'a babel of creeds in the same school'. These new 'schools existed to serve society by tending to the characters of otherwise neglected children' (p. 32). The poor must attend. Attitude formation via a carefully-structured system of content, pedagogy and organization was to be their reward. The educational 'movement' of people like Bernard and Mann produced by mid-century the abolition of district power in favour of the board run, free, public, largely co-educational, curriculum-differentiated (into classical and non-classical) High School. Efficiency grounded 'classification of scholars' was a pressure from the start as schools served economic change by shifting ascription (an emphasis on who children were by background) to achievement (an emphasis on what they could do). The superintendent system, coupled with the development of normal schools for training and teacher professionalization generally 'became an intimate aspect of bureaucratic strategy' (p. 36).

Minority sensibilities required the school to be religiously and politically neutral. In practice a 'tepid Protestant tone', devoted to sublimation was, if anything, more pervasive than the class bias. According to Katz, he sees irony in the vision of schoolmen who thought that they were promoting a *common* school when rejecting localism on the ostensible grounds of inefficiency and interference with parental rights, when usually it stemmed 'from a gut fear of the cultural divisiveness inherent in the increasing religious and ethnic diversity of American life ... Bureaucracy was intended to standardize far more than the conduct of public life' (p. 39). Thus, 'racism' the invidious ranking of cultural diversity via the assumption of the desirability of homogenization (O! twentieth-century definition) was there from the start. The poor, not easily initially attracted in large numbers, were blamed from the start for bureaucratic inefficiency. The interest of the middle class lay both in a pedagogy rooted in the arousal of interest and affection and 'the success of universal, elaborate, graded school systems' (p. 51). Fear of the proletariat came to the same thing in the sense that it could be responded to via the same school reflex. Organization mediated between change and structure. There is visible play between the growing articulation of class-based interests and educational structure and process. The school system described by Katz at one and the same time provided pedagogical and evaluatory devices, hand tooled to maximizing their 'take' from the class originating them, while containing and filtering the energies of those more subservient. All this could be justified in terms of an open and rescuing ethic. Gently treated and well-graded child-grains come to finer flower. Bureaucracy came with egalitarian intent and stayed for class-based, inegalitarian regulatory ends. Class pedagogy as described by Bernstein was not born yesterday.

We cannot dwell on Katz's account of how full scale bureaucratization based explicitly on productive industry models came piecemeal to Boston between 1851–76, or why by the early seventies it was under vigorous attack by reformers who found it tightly knit enough to withstand them and the individual charismatics hired to alter it. But by the eighties it was perfected and spreading elsewhere. It could resist community pressure, enshrining order, efficiency and uniformity in preference to responsiveness, variety and flexibility. It easily withstood the early twentieth-century pressure of 'progressivism', which Katz sees anyway as a variety of inherently conservative change forces concerning control, management, philosophy and pedagogy, whose essentially order-oriented nature fitted in well with the pattern of unequal sorting mechanisms of a bureaucratic structure. Dewey becomes all too easily the *eminence grise* of the 'corporate state'.

The cult of efficiency

Political and educational progressivism and the pursuit of efficiency are very much the themes of other recent American educational historians. Callahan shows how in the period 1910–29, the 'incipient bureaucracy' which Katz argues had won the day by the 1880s, came to full fruition by the widespread adoption of business values and practices by American educational administrators. Their extreme vulnerability to business ideology stemmed all too easily from local support and control, especially financial, which geared response to the origin of criticism rather than to its intrinsic merit.

Callahan shows that by the first decade of this century, most city school boards, paralleling a more general municipal reform movement, had ceased to be 'large unwieldly organizations governed to some extent by politics', and had become much smaller and composed of 'businessmen who were to run the schools along business lines' (p. 7). The identifications of career administrators thus changed from the scholastic and the statesmanlike to the businesslike. A growing belief in relevant and practical curricular and cost effectiveness, against the background of the immigrant explosion, already marked the ethos assaulted in 1910 by Leonard Ayre's study showing substantial 'retardation' (i.e. children over-age for their grade) in schools, and advocating the use of an 'Index of Efficiency' focussing on grade 'repeaters'.

This 'exposure' coincided with the railroad finance investigation which brought Frederick W. Taylor to prominence, whose 'scientific management', originally inspired by time and motioning the Dutchman Schmidt to shift 48 rather than

$12\frac{1}{2}$ tons of pig-iron per day at Bethlehem Steel, promised to increase wages *and* cut costs. Taylor's own argument was 'that his principles could be "applied with equal force to all activities"' (Callahan, p. 43) – homes, farms, churches or wherever. In an atmosphere of mounting criticism in the media of schools and their performance administrators took, in the period around 1912, to the 'efficiency gospel'.

Its educational version had two major manifestations: firstly, the ethic of plant and resource utilization and, secondly, efficiency measures for pupils and teaching via tests of achievement and later IQ. By 1913, arithmetic, handwriting and English scales were in 'wide currency' and work to improve them carried on in universities and full-time 'efficiency bureaus'. Attempts to rate teachers were also a major venture, and spread to other education-employed personnel, too.

The motives of administrators in introducing such measures were, according to Callahan, primarily those of self-defence of legitimacy and resources. Surveys of school systems by outside 'experts' became universal for the same reasons, but tended to have the unhappy effect of emphasizing the financial and mechanical aspect of things in a way which mere educators found it difficult to challenge. Callahan harshly indicts the lack of resistance or quality of criticism displayed by most relevant university educators. With few exceptions (such as Dewey), they joined the Taylorian rush. Educational administration as professional study was very much founded in such an atmosphere.

The high-water mark of the 'movement' was, in Callahan's terms, the establishment of the 'Platoon school'. It originated in the Gary Plan, introduced in 1908 by Wirt, one of Dewey's ex-students. Its essence was to enrich 'the regular academic program by connecting it with nature study, art, music and industrial education ... and still be economical' (p. 129). To this end, students moved from room to room at bell-time (requiring a great deal of organization in the large schools of Gary, Indiana), thus ensuring constant use of special facilities. The plan became widely discussed after 1915, and was in use in 632 schools in 126 cities by 1925, 1068 schools in 202 cities by 1929, involving three-quarters of a million pupils.

Whereas by 1915, the extravagance of Wirt had 'plunged the Gary schools into debt ...' (the appeal of the idea to modern ears is instantaneous, and its expense surely an intrinsic plus sign!), New York was taking up the plan experimentally. It was immediately attacked for being a system of economics rather than education, clearly getting caught up in the politics of graft and shortage of the era. It became associated with shift-system schooling and Wirt, who was invited to come to apply it to New York schools, had to say, despite his previous claims to the contrary, that he was 'not specially interested in running school systems cheaply' (p. 141).

Whatever the merits or demerits of versions of the Gary Plan (and Callahan is far from decisive in his own judgement), it is clear that the efficiency movement transformed the American superintendent from educator to administrator, and led to tremendous emphasis on demonstrating efficiency through records and reports and cost accounting. Perhaps the most important element in the educational balance sheet was, as Callahan suggests, 'child accounting'. The *economic motivation to promote students, plus the practice of rating the efficiency of teachers on the basis of promotions* created *two potent forces ... which contributed to the practice of passing students regardless of educational considerations* (p. 168, his italics). The increasing size and what Callahan calls the 'service station ethic' of schools were oriented to the same end, produced by men who approached 'education in a businesslike, mechanical, organization way. They saw nothing wrong with imposing impossible loads on high school teachers, because they were not students or scholars and did not understand the need for study and preparation' (p. 247). They were equally likely to run a college in the same spirit.

Pleasing the Corporate State

Spring's view of the system is end-on with this. 'Since 1900 the power of schooling has tended to be in the hands of businessmen, political leaders and professional educators who have been instrumental in the development of the modern corporate state' (p. 149). He forms this view by exploring 'the exact meaning Progressives gave to public education during its most formative period at the beginning of the twentieth century'. Progressives are defined as 'those American leaders who adopted as the image of the good society a highly organized and smoothly working corporate structure' (p. xi). They were leaders of labour, as well as corporations, financiers, politicians, philosophers and educators, whose views were formative of public education which set out to group-train and vocationally guide students in their image. 'Individualizing instruction' really meant rooting out 'selfish individualism' as preparation for filling social roles.

This takes place within the 'corporate state', set amid the urban growth and crowded despair at the turn of the century, where *laissez-faire* steadily lost out to the economics of scale. It was the period of the emergence of large labour unions and corporate monopolies, where Gompers could envisage co-operative harmony via the checks and balances of large-scale trusts, labour unions and consumer organizations; and Perkins could depict the modern corporation, made inevitable by technology, suitably government regulated, as the means of reaching co-operative society (we might call it America's Mitsubishi Twitch). This sort of social ethic, Spring points out, reached its fullest political expression in the campaign of Theodore Roosevelt's Progressive Party in 1912, devoted publicly not to rooting out corporations but only their evil aspects.

The large corporation, Spring suggests, was already highly conscious of the usefulness of, and was adept at organizing, employee welfare programmes (including educational ones), not least as anti-union insurance. Within education the drill-like classroom, along with grades and rewards, came under fire for inculcating rigidity and unselfishness. Group work as popularized by Dewey and others was seen as the answer. Dewey's broad vision to use the classroom to 'give meaning to the fragmented experiences of the world of modern man' (p. 54), lost freshness when combined with the more directive 'self-organized group' work of Scott, his contemporaneously well-known Bostonian antagonist. Social understanding gave way to 'social like-mindedness', reflecting highly organized society's needs – 'Motivation and rewards were to become contingent on the approval of others' (p. 61).

At the level of school organization, real attempts were made to extend the long-standing social role tradition of the school towards 'social centres' with reform intentions. Frequently, however, they were only recreational, and ran counter to the logics of moves away from local political control and the crystallizing professional bureaucracy noted earlier. The major surviving response to corporate society's needs from the first decade of the century, was the establishment of vocational guidance and junior-high schools. The junior-high's original purpose was to enable 'vocational' guidance to happen early. This in its turn gave way to 'educational' guidance and counselling in both the homeroom and by specialists. The junior-highs offered differentiated courses and groupings to help develop adolescent social instincts in the context of de-mocracy defined as 'doing that which you were best able to' (p. 107).

Specialization and socialization thus stood in tension, lead-ing to the formation of the comprehensive high school, where the extra-curricular and student involvement in government was expected to do much to achieve a balance between them. In effect – 'Educators were often so concerned about the need for a particular well-rounded personality that they put social training before the academic' (p. 125). School's use of a variety of means as controlling institutions prepared the individual to accept distinctive forms of power particularly connected with obedience to capitalistic leaders and the legitimacy of meri-tocracy. Thus, they tended 'to reinforce and strengthen exist-ing social structures and social stratification' (p. 151). We shall see this echoed by Coleman's study conducted in the 1950s.

Spring's conclusion is nothing if not definite: 'Dependence upon institutions and expertise presents a form of alienation which goes far beyond anything suggested by Karl Marx in the nineteenth century' (p. 153). 'The school increases this alienation by making alien the very ability of the individual to act or create. In the nineteenth century man lost the product of his labour; in the twentieth century he lost his will' (p. 154). As enslavement to technology increases, 'happiness' becomes the increasing responsibility of education and vocational guidance its arch-villain. The nineteenth-century belief that education was the most human form of social control, despite its surface democracy, has become doubly dangerous – 'children are taught to feel free even though their lives are being directed by institutional forces' (p. 163). Spring's literate rhetoric drives him to the necessity of the abolition of the power of the school.

Do two rhetorics make a truth?

The contributions of 'critical historians' like Katz and Spring to our understanding of education as social control are both refreshing and disturbing. Their verbal and analytical violence is certainly useful in shaking an endemic mood which sees education as simply beneficence. At the same time, their failure to deal with or to bring out fully enough certain features of their topic of concern is especially odd, given their anti-authority and debunking tone. One could detail this in several respects, for instance in relation to their neglect of the cyclical nature of progressive educational views of 'best practice', as demonstrated by Cremin (1961); or, even more generally, in their failure to examine the cultural functions of education other than as unilateral class domination. I would wish to exempt Callahan's rather more proper historical delimitation of his area from the force of these strictures, though even he falls into the trap of underemphasis of awkward portions of the evidence. For example, it is difficult to gain any directly inferrable sense from his work of where the efficiency ethic failed to penetrate the American educational world.

Having said all this, and in a sense it amounts to no more than the (eminently and necessitously reversible) notion that one should watch out most for the rhetorical predelictions of those who most hunt them down in others, this work has direct virtue in respect of our concern. Katz does show how even a few people can articulate and institutionalize in classrooms and school evaluatory and organizational procedures, principles congenial to some social groups and, at least in part, controlling and repressing in terms of the characteristics of others. This is a theme which will recur throughout the rest of this book. Callahan shows how ideas and beliefs in one area of society can spread to and dominate politically inferior social regions and, as in the case of the American attainment testing vogue after the First World War, can thoroughly colour and reinforce conceptions of ability and progress. Spring, despite his lapses into vituperation and selective emphasis, strongly suggests how and why economic and business needs percolate into educational organizations as shaping and preparing agencies. What he and others tend to lack is grasp of the fact that economic surplus creates the possibility for greater altruism as well as a greater complexification of the process of social control. Conspiracies aim to hide more subtly but do not necessarily grow more efficient in culturally less simple societies.

IQ – the test of bondage

If Spring is not a high scorer on care over proceeding from stated objectives to realized events (the basis of his rhetoric appears at times to be a perfect credulity about words being as good as deeds), the balance is tipped even further by Karier who most fully represents the fashion for casting testing as the current *bête noir* of liberationists (Karier, 1972). He makes great play of the connections between the origins of the IQ testing movement and eugenics (so that one feels just *once* like saying that Plato believed in slavery, Hegel the Prussian state, Marx sanctioned class-slaughter and Wittgenstein was a pederast) on both sides of the Atlantic via Galton, Goddard, Terman, Thorndike and the like. (Binet, for the record, was a noteable dissenter.) Karier argues that the backdrop to the emergence of the testing movement was the rapid increase in corporate capital and immigration in America (also for the record, British Galton wanted to know about genius, while Binet had a worry or two about Parisian children). By the period of the First World War, when mass-schooling and the corporate, liberal state were firmly established, techniques were available to apply to 1·7 million men in the US army, and the lessons learned incorporated in tests widely available and applied to the post-war school system.

In the educational atmosphere of the twenties described by Callahan, against the backdrop of what Karier refers to as the temperance and cleansing *zeitgeist*, the socially and racially biased tests (e.g. Stanford Binet) began the formation of the lower class American adult who has become 'a product of fifty years of testing. He has been channelled through an intricate bureaucratic educational system which in the name of meeting his individual needs, classified and tracked him into an occupation appropriate to his socio-economic status' (p. 167). The tests themselves have become a vital part of the American social infrastructure and our man a tragic figure who has internalized their message for him. Jensen's definition of the meaning of IQ as 'something like the probability of acceptable performance (given the opportunity) in occupations varying in social standing' (quoted p. 168, from Jensen, 1969: 14) confirms for him, given the *lack* of equal opportunity, their class and racist bias. 'Tracking' in high school, spreading since the twenties, declared a violation of rights in a 1967 Washington court decision without effect, is their organizational concomitant, no doubt helping the tests to 'effectively immobilize any real revolutionary opposition'. The power of human invention is fertile but we shall have cause later to ask whether American 'contest mobility' was ever as simple as this.

Meanwhile we must also point up the question raised earlier when discussing the role of objective tests in the changing pattern of British educational opportunity, as to whether IQ measuring can be castigated as easily as this. It may well be that the American experience of putting IQ to the use of demonstrating or confirming racial (cultural, political and economic) inferiority has a peculiarly poignant smack. But test bias aside – and historically it is *bias* and not exclusion – the bad use to which testing has been put has to be weighed against testing as irrestistible evidence of brightness, even among the lower orders. Control via the internalized message of low IQ (or association with those guilty of such) is a cultural fact and its technicist rudeness may be worse than bad luck. But it really is absurd of Karier and others to extrude the doubts of 1970 on to the events of half a century ago which were pursued in quite a different logic. It is even less considered to argue as if the question of 'tracking' (what we would call streaming or setting) in schools is at all straightforward or clarified as an educational problem. A credible case might

indeed be argued for the proposition that whatever the consequences of differentiation within education (upon motivation), any attempt to abolish or reduce it (in the interests of
motivation), actually enhances the necessity to somehow record difference, at least until we are sure that the trams keep
on running and that their drivers do not necessarily inherit
their occupation.

The case of the misplaced endogenous variable

Plenty, but we can't get no satisfaction

Ideas about the relationship between the means of educational
production and revolutionary consciousness are more fully
developed by the Marxist economist, Gintis. He argues that
modern economic 'neo-classical theory has a great deal of
explaining to do. The growth of capitalism exhibits the
bureaucratization and fragmentation of work, the destruction
of communities, the elimination of healthy and aesthetic environments, irrational military expenditure and war, repressive educational systems, substantial inequality of income,
wealth and power, and a passive, fetishistic, status oriented
stance of individuals vis-à-vis marketable commodities'
(1972b).

In economists' terms (who said it can't be fun?), Gintis believes that neo-classical theory cannot begin to analyse the
malaise, for it casts peoples' preferences or tastes as *exogenous*
to its system of variables, i.e. quantities and prices of goods are
related to each other and to other prices, incomes, costs and so
on *but* the basic state of what consumers 'like' and what they
'are like' is taken as *given*. Gintis' contention is that even when
these economists shift so as to recognize that firms create and
manipulate demand and markets, their analysis still lacks the
power to reveal what Marx analysed as alienation.

In capitalist production, choices must be consistent with its
social relations. Individuals may *want* good work, etc., but they
only *need* more consumption. Education in particular ensures
that humans are shaped so that 'workers' preferences are *endogenous to the production process*' (1972b: 271): that is,

their tastes and aspirations, their inclinations and needs are tailored to man the machines and consume their products. We have a school system where 'youth "put up with the classroom shit" in anticipation of higher income', and get hooked on the process (1970: 41). Economists of education who pursue the relationship between earnings and education, controlling (or allowing) analytically for IQ or achievement differences are proceeding on a false premise. School matters but not in that respect.

Repression, reproduction and the 'new class'

Gintis argues that the function of education in any society is much as Parsons and Inkeles have revealed it: to produce humans socialized into appropriate values and bearing requisite competencies. Capitalistic techniques are highly developed – 'the educational system tends to become functionally reduced to its role in generating labour for the economy and the development of the individual becomes more or less fully tailored to the needs of "economic rationality"' (1970: 29). As Dreeben describes, the specialized system 'structures motivation' by (except in the case of a few categories of workers), moulding personality repressively in the light of the needs of bureaucracy. Indeed, *education is productive only insofar as it is repressive*' (1970: 34) in respect of the subordination, discipline and the level of cognitive orientation necessary in modern economic process.

The 'perfected' worker appears to be the most highly educated, who in terms of the Marxian dialectic must therefore be the most 'opposed' in terms of true interests to the system. Gintis' belief is that educated labour – whose objective level tends to be similar in economic systems at comparable, high levels of development – is the new 'emergent' class, capable of replacing the old proletariat: 'the effective interests of educated labour are opposed to the capitalistic institutions and the development of radical consciousness will be facilitated by the instrumental role of youth and student power, as direct participants at the point of generation of educated labour' (1970: 20–1).

All this must be set against the 'dialectic of economic

growth', the cornerstone of socialist consciousness in developed, high growth societies. 'Growth in material production, the keynote of capitalist economic activity, is itself the catalyst of socialist consciousness' (1970: 37). The modern key contradiction of capitalism is revealed as its inexorable pressure towards continued expansion of GNP, facilitated by the successful inculcation by the education and familial systems of the requisite attributes in individuals, except that the 'internalization of individual consumption orientation fails to be a "self-fulfilling prophecy"' (1970: 41). In its reproductive provision, the 'socialization of commodity fetishism' is reconfirmed in a vital way every day by society which originally 'cybernetically patterns' human orientations in education. But yet mass-consuming society fails to satisfy the individual. Indeed Gintis argues that if the aesthetic and spiritual capacities of the mass of citizens were highly developed capitalism would likely survive only a short time. What power or principality would not sensibly tremble?

It is not at all difficult to see why Gintis diagnoses Illich's view of modern education as consumer-orientated, as inadequate, and why he would not on Marxist premises favour deschooling (1972a). His positive view of human nature and happiness has much to do with an 'early Marxist' view of post-capitalist, post-alienative freedom for de-specialized and humanly actualized man. He frequently enjoins his educated readers to join in and help with the work of socialist reconstruction, which involves accepting, in American milieux, an 'outlaw' position. He has high expectation of the affluent young's powers of rejection of their on-going alienation. But we are left a little hazy, apart from the pleasures of the dialectic, as to what comes next except the millenial fusing of the contradictions. We shall find that Bourdieu has a thing or two to say below about cultural capital and reproduction which make the shackles look a trifle tighter.

Scarce resources, which have alternate uses

Gintis is an entirely literate neo-classical economist who has elected to speak another language, on account of the inadequacy of the mother tongue. Fluent native-speakers of

EconoEd would meet him with all sorts of tightly argued rejoinders about deficiencies in his arguments, ranging from how in fact tastes are complexified in terms of modern welfare economics, through to the empirical daftness about the argument about the contradictions between growing GNP (*per se*) and personal discontent. There is a limit, however, to how far the traditional economist could or would meet his value-laden Marxist and revolutionary views, for the classical economic tradition has built its reputation on a functional repugnance of 'value' issues and has managed with an entirely vestigial model of man. These are its strengths rather than weaknesses.

Bowles, in opposition, but in terms of his writings where he is still working within it, displays a more than usual attention to the limitations of the traditional assumptions of stage-like growth and the reciprocal relation of education to economic development, until the point arrives where the 'spread of mass education, *ipso facto*, is regarded as evidence of growth' (1969: 5). Planning education to maximize resource efficiency and to avoid bottlenecks becomes normal, its need arising 'largely from the peculiar characteristics of the production process of schools and the consumption of their outputs' (1969: 11). School output is multi-dimensional and schooling-earnings relations have a variety of origins. More may bring more simply because employers assume that it should, 'income' measures may be self-confirming in respect of education-productivity, or may, *à la* Gintis, have sources other than the extra school years of educands. However, Bowles believes that the Gintis view does not fundamentally damage the economic case that employers tend towards 'conscious optimization ... of relative factor productivities' (p. 24), i.e. pay for what they get, even if it is only 'trainability' or some such capacity.

Education production has peculiar features. Techniques are much the same everywhere, but resources cannot easily be changed in use. The process is extremely lengthy and the parts of the system – one bit's outputs are another's inputs – are highly interdependent. As buildings and personnel tend to be highly specific and the prejudice against the market mechanism great, cost and output planning errors tend also to be great. The potential 'disequilibria' effect on institutions and people (of over and under supply) are so severe that there is universal pressure to organize education as a system. We can take this in its own right – the creation of a machine to render a stable though differentiated educational product for economic ends – as the backdrop to social control. The machine may be put to alternative uses.

Upon which the sun never sets

Carnoy is quite sure that the machine is at least multifunctional. Competitive schooling makes capitalist sense, demeaning children by building only upon what they bring, 'colonizing' people into acceptance of the status quo. Though a few poor may, importantly, via education reach dissent and radical thinking 'these are not the *primary purposes* ... of school systems' (1974: 13). Schooling has brought people out of traditional hierarchy and put them into a capitalist one of greater working and social dependency. As has been the case with colonial regimes, the success of whose educational system is 'attested' by their continuance under their new masters, so school too is a *colonizer* within Western powers. It attempts 'to impose economic and political relationships in the society *especially* on those children who gain least (or lose most) from those relationships', expecting children to accept 'unstatisfactory roles'. One class can colonize another: men, women; whites, blacks, etc. 'all *within* an imperial nation' (1974: 19), hence the 'national independence' attribute of some of the subnational freedom movements, requiring psychological as well as political unyoking.

We cannot possibly do justice to the quality of Carnoy's work here on metropolitan and non-western development. It has all the freshness and power of *exposé*, giving hero-status to the traditionally oppressed, as well as the defects of the rhetoric of one side of the struggle. Which side is clear enough and we can read for sense, as well as emotion, right on. He is not alone among the 'political economists' in showing us that a little learning is dangerous. But what about the stink of ignorance? We know the failure of school half accomplished. But where can school be fully accomplished? In apartheid enclave? Carnoy believes that a 'reconstructed society may emerge after a long period of violent revolution or may be built democratically' (1974: 367), but we are not told whether it is to be a society of Freirian *epimethian* saints, where knowledge has been cut down to the convenient size chunks that do not get between people, or of Mao or ...? He certainly believes that a reconstructed society – 'a society in *continuous liberation* – will be one where 'education organized in schools may indeed be an inherently colonizing institution' and that in the move towards it 'free' or 'liberation' schools may be vital breakdown mechanisms.

Now you see it – no you'd better not!

I do not know how many of the political economists would plead the exigencies of the revolution(s) over scholarship, but it is difficult to find in any of them evidence for altruism or disinterest anywhere in the present or historic past of education. They might indeed claim agnosticism about knowing the power of knowledge freed from hierarchical structures (would it take a Mannheim to do the boys' work?) as the rises of the twin gods of schooling and class society have taken place simultaneously. And as we have seen, they claim scripture for the evil powers of testing, taking Jencks in their stride. Bowles and Gintis (1974) say in effect that if everyone was equally 'bright' as measured by tests, there would be little change in the extent to which sons ended up doing the same sorts of jobs as their fathers. This is not an altogether unreasonable comment on the complex debate as rendered by Jencks *et alia*, but remember that *all* sorts of statements are reasonable in the light of its statistical evidence (e.g. see Jencks *et al.* 1972: 318) on occupation–IQ–income–schooling linkage within and between generations. It is now a widely held piece of the *faith* that primary blame for economic inequality cannot be laid upon genetic difference in IQ scores, status inheritance or schools – 'Economic success seems to depend upon varieties of luck and on-the-job competence' (p. 8) only 'moderately related' to these factors. Job competence varies widely but seems to depend more on personality than skills. Strategies for equalizing competence, more so luck, are hard to conceive. Neither inequality nor poverty is inevitable, but schooling would not rate highly among strategies for their removal.

Bowles puts the simplistic case for the opposition nicely: under capitalism schooling disequalizes income distribution even in the absence of social class: assume as the economists say, only two factors of production: capital, unequally distributed, and labour, uneducated and undifferentiated. Let the labour skills be randomly distributed. Initially 'the only source of income inequality in this society is the unequal distribution of capital'. Let there now be schooling to differentiate labour by itself or type of skill – 'unequalities of labour earnings' now augment 'the unequalities inherent in the concentration of capital' (1975: 56). Schooling would pile on to capital so that 'substantial negative correlation' between them would soon be required to ensure equality. But a vogue for compensation notwithstanding, education was never like this in the sense of offering to them that hath less. Bowles, in fact, settles for a particularly crude picture of 'class culture' mechanism to ensure hopelessness – 'the children of managers and professionals are taught self-reliance within a broad set of constraints; the children of production workers are taught obedience' (p. 59). Why do both radicals and conservatives need the same image of *the* working and middle classes? How dare they persist in it in the face of research that shows as much intra- as inter-'class' difference along so many dimensions? Come home Melvin Kohn, we know you found this out but told us different; all is forgiven; we'll sit down and read your small print together. We'll find it especially poignant that those who see the working class as the harbinger of the bright future, most believe in its ability to be disabled.

In this view even 'testing' has to retreat a few steps as villain to be replaced by school as the 'channelling colony' where the lower class of equal 'abilities' have been historically differentially labelled in the name of science via unfair tests so as to be processed by a system which they were unable to resist on account of their obedient class culture. But whatever happened to the reality of that slowly-changing, mature occupational structure? It is much easier to demonstrate that education helps in getting a better paying job than that it contributes to productivity. 'Human capital' analysis may be rational explanation in pursuit of (collectively) irrational behaviour. But even if businessmen and governments are irrational in their employment policies, individuals are not irrational in pursuing job-valued education. We cannot anyway test this wholesale, but only point to its reality at the margin or via absurd case. However, we can say with complete certainty that for any given school generation, *qua* generation, the occupation structure is pretty determinate. 'Good jobs' are not there for all. The system, like a cruel sponge, soaks up excess qualification in inflated job-price. The school, in this sense, is a 'channelling colony'; but so is anything, potentially, that precedes job-entry.

Given this, we can work out some intimations of possible social alternatives. The chances of institutionalizing social *potlatch* are not and never were high. That annually, decennially or whenever a society should burn or consume to destruction its occupational goods, following this with some sort of vocational raffle, hardly accords with anything that we know about anthropological, economic or social possibility. The links between the material, social, cultural and personality aspects of society seem to need to be stabler than that, though clearly not as ossified as they have been in many historical situations, including our own.

The further alternatives appear to be therefore either some species of alternation of role systems (like Marx's 1844 vision of 'communist' society or, presumably, Illich's 'conviviality') which might be accomplished either on the basis of massive withdrawal from *or* some sort of technologized perfecting of mass-productive modes; or a revision of social ranking systems and their underlying criteria, so that jobs go on for ever, but their meaning is transformed. This latter is the clear achievement of existing Marxist–Leninist–Maoist revolutions, East and West, in varying degree (the Maoist one also showing us that occupational echelons other than owners can be excised or transformed, at some considerable system-shock requiring strong countervailing force). Such change will of course have potentially profound effect on human dignity as well as economic relations. That it creates differently favoured and disfavoured categories, and has implications for pluralistic knowledge conceptions also goes without saying.

Whatever the judgement about the balance of these issues, there is no doubt that the discovery and institutionalization of 'one best way' for society increases the salience of the system of induction into it (certainly in the short run and when there is still 'heresy' about) including schooling. Where there *is* consensus about a 'central value system' as is currently more the case in Marxist (as historically in theocratic or Fascist) societies than in pluralistic ones, then doubt about control in its name is weakened. To understand Marx, we must turn to Durkheim, for ideologies and class dominances, like Empires, come and go, but society goes on for ever. The necessities of the social transcend those of class or economics even in those societies where it seems suffused by production and production-based hierarchy. We should try to clarify some of these relations in the next two chapters by looking more closely at original and present-day versions of these great traditions as they apply to education.

5

Two great sociologies, both of necessity: Marx and Durkheim

Durkheim's 'political economy'

Past is present

As Professor of Sociology and Education, a great deal of Durkheim's work comes to us in the form of published lectures. They differ a good deal in terms of their intended audience. To his graduate secondaries, he delivered *The Evolution of Educational Theory in France*. He goes directly to what is topical – the reforms then under debate, which he sees as particularly difficult in secondary schools, where many teach differing subjects. He advocates the virtue of inspecting the past for the clarification of the present crisis (like our critical historians after him) both to illustrate that the meaning of education depends on age, stage and destiny, and that systems are the result of 'specific and mutually interacting social forces' (1976: Ch. 1), there being no immutable form as there is no immutable society. Organizations and the 'model of man which ... education must seek to construct' (1976: Ch. 1) are capable of historical illumination.

Modern man, he argues, is not simply an agglomeration of present traits: 'in each one of us, in differing degrees is contained the person we were yesterday ...'. Indeed, it dominates us and we only indirectly feel the influence of 'these past selves precisely because they are deeply rooted within us'. They are our unconscious past and we tend 'to ignore their legitimate demands' (1976: Ch. 1).

Historical study may also help us to realize that new (including educational) theories are always violently aggressive to those which they may seek to replace. Rousseau, for example, was unhappy about too little spontaneity, so he made 'a systematically negative methodology the one essential feature of any sound educational theory ...' declaring 'education through contact with natural phenomena the exclusive basis for any education whatsoever' (1976: Ch. 2).

Sacred and profane: a whole child is better than none

Secondary education was of special importance in the French system. Its 'initial germ' lay back beyond the Renaissance and the Scholastics, in the meeting between the intensely alien Frankish barbarians and Rome, mediated between by the Church, with education providing the means for transfusing its life force. Remarkably, it was the 'astringent joys of renunciation', unsurprisingly appealing to weary Rome, which also engaged the simple barbarians and answered their needs and aspirations. Culture came as a corollary of the faith.

The Church had its scruples about, but could not dispense with, Graeco-Roman profanity. Latin was necessary and the faith involved imbibing ideas. Teaching and preaching, books and linguistic skills, history and rhetoric, were indispensable. *Convicts* were church schools in cathedral environments where pagan culture had perforce to be studied. Watching over the salvation of humanity led on to tending it, and the monastic orders followed into schooling. From cathedral and cloister the whole system emerged: sacred over against profane, teacher as priest.

Durkheim notes a contradiction built into the embryo, between pagan and christian, secular and religious, as 'a phenomenon which dominates the whole of our academic and educational development'. He also notes that in antiquity, the pupil 'went to a teacher of grammar or letters in order to learn grammar, to the teacher of the other to learn music, to the rhetorician to learn rhetoric, etc. ... All these different forms of teaching met together inside him but outwardly they were isolated. It was a mosaic of different types of teaching which were only formally collected'. In the first Christian schools, exactly the opposite obtained. 'All the teaching which took place in them was given in one and the same place and was consequently subjected to one and the same influence, tended in one and the same moral direction' (1976: Ch. 2). Performance of pupil–teacher relationships and the unity of Christian doctrine characterized the experience. The school took over the child in its entirety and provided for all its needs. Christian awareness was of the need to create within a man 'a general disposition of the mind and the will which will make him see things in general in a particular light' (1976: Ch. 3), the nurturing of 'a certain attitude of the soul ... a certain *habitus* of our moral being' became the essential aim of education, the alternative route to conversion to a state of grace. Durkheim believed that a secularized version of the same aim still dominated education in his day – morally cohesive, conducted in schools viewed as communities.

Seven forms

We lack the space to follow in any detail how Durkheim develops his account of the medieval and subsequent development of French schooling. It is of particular interest to note that for many hundreds of years human knowledge divided into seven branches of seven fundamental disciplines, the trivium of grammar, rhetoric and dialectic and the quadrivium, composed of geometry, arithmetic, astronomy and music. The former were about the mind and thinking itself and dealt with reasoning and language. The latter group dealt with things, the real world. They furnish the origin of our continuing curricular split – humanities and natural science, and 'the realities to which they give expression' (1976: Ch. 4). At the beginning, the quadrivium was regarded as *de luxe* and rather magical. 'For centuries it seemed self-evident that only studies relating to human beings could really serve to shape human beings' with grammar, as maximum generality, predominating. Indeed, grammar became cult; mistakes in authoritative texts had to be shown to be only apparent, riddles became high taste until developments in rhetoric and dialectic came to the rescue.

The grammatical curriculum was not without value in Durkheim's view for grammar disinterred the immanent logic of a language and put it on display: 'language is not some sort of an external garment in which thought is clothed from the outside, without any really satisfactory fit being possible. The truth is that language is a far more integrated element in human thought. It renders it possible no less than it presupposes it. Without language thought would remain at the lowest levels; for none of the even remotely complex forms of mental life could have established themselves without the use of words ... the study of language is, if one knows how to set about it, to study thought itself' (1976: Ch. 5). It led on naturally to questions of ontology (the really real). The scholastic obsession was with the problem of universals − 'what do the words mean which express general and abstract ideas?' (1976: Ch. 5) Durkheim argues that realism was the initial 'natural mode of thought', where kinds *did* have a real existence, it could be held that white is a substance like table and that logically, the non-existent actually exists. His belief was that it required a more sophisticated, later (post medieval) mind to prise an object away from the qualities which it might possess.

Flexible though balanced people

Durkheim's historical search for the material bases of human knowledge and schooling led him to the not surprising view that secondary education designed vocationally was 'radically incoherent'. Theoretically the problem was 'knowing towards what kinds of things the pupil's thinking should be directed'. The answer to this he saw as quite inescapably shaped by the fact that 'there are two and only two main types of thing which are possible objects of thought; human phenomena and natural phenomena' (1976: Ch. 12). 'Far from being immutable, humanity is in fact involved in an interminable process of evolution, disintegration and reconstruction ... History teaches us that there are as many different types of moral systems as there are different types of society ... an expression of the great diversity of circumstances under which collective living takes place' (1976: Ch. 12). Even Oedipus sometimes hides.

The *diversity* of human nature needed to become the basic subject matter of the humanities in education, not as anthropological titillation, but presented so as to help resist the deep-rooted feeling that true humanity emerges only in certain civilizations. 'In the myths, legend and skills of even the most primitive peoples there are involved highly complex mental processes which sometimes shed more light on the mechanisms of the human mind, than the more self-conscious intellectual operations on which the positive sciences are based.' We cannot say of *any* point in history 'here is manifested the essence of human nature'; it becomes, 'illegitimate for us to assign a limit in advance to what man is capable of producing in future, or to assume that a time will come when man's capacity for creative innovation being exhausted, he will be doomed to repeat himself throughout all eternity' (1976: Ch. 12). Man is an infinitely flexible, protean force. Such education will enable him to conceive of different principles of ethical and moral order, without risking neophobic retrenchment or arbitrary change: 'all change, in colliding with the inherited institutions of the past, is inevitably hard and laborious; consequently it only takes place in response to the demands of necessity' (1976: Ch. 12) and requires the overcoming of a whole network of diverse casual relationships.

Moreover, modern psychology, according to Durkheim, confirmed that 'other', 'unfamiliar' men live in us. We have 'an unconscious psychic life beyond that of consciousness'. To achieve self-consciousness and knowing activity 'we must treat ourselves as an unknown quantity, whose nature and character we must seek to grasp by examining – as is the case with external objects – the objective phenomena which express it and not by giving heed to those so transitory and unreliable impressions of inner feelings' (1976: Ch. 12). For the moment, history (destined to merge with a sufficiently developed psychological-social science), would have to be the chief vehicle of curricular renewal.

The child, society and knowledge

Starting from where it is and they are

Durkheim's much more fully known work on education consists of his lectures given to primary teachers in 1902–3 (*Moral Education*) and collection of assorted articles and lectures published between 1902–6 (*Education and Sociology*). Both first appeared in English translation in the twenties and it is not difficult to see how the guy with the funny ideas about group mind fell outside the sympathies of American educators with the characteristics depicted by the 'political economists' above. The American emphasis on the individual child stemmed, it is often said, from 'the frontier', Protestant theology and the psychology-testing monopoly of educational theory and practice. Durkheim's conception of the purpose of education was dramatically different: 'a social means to a social end – the means by which a society guarantees its own survival' (Wilson, in Durkheim, 1961: xiii), through the production of moral beings in consensus. We have already noted that by 'moral' Durkheim means 'social', not 'ethical'. But of course ethics, being part of society, would have a 'moral' force – not so much *double entendre* as indissolubility! Durkheim's impetus comes from Kant, indeed his whole sociology can be read as an attempt to demonstrate, metaphysics apart, the sociality and social necessity of Kant's principles (Durkheim, 1961: 108–10 for discussion).

In this light, then, we should read that individual morality involved consistency or regularity of conduct and a sense of authority (both aspects of discipline), impersonality of orientation ('. . . the domain of moral begins where the domain of the social begins') and autonomy. As with Kant, the categorical nature of moral imperatives is softened in the fully developed being; not only should we learn to kiss the hand that strikes us and wish such treatment in like case for ourselves and others, but we should learn how and when to deflect the blow. For

Durkheim regularity, discipline, group orientation *and* autonomy could exist via 'reliable knowledge'. 'The difference between self-determination and witless submission lies in the ability to predict accurately the consequences of alternative courses of action' (Wilson, Durkheim, 1961: xii), in terms of a science of 'morality'. The opening up of moral life to rationality constituted a decisive move in favour of open-endedness, whose consequences for individuals and society could not be calculated – 'a given advance in moral education in the direction of greater rationality cannot occur without bringing to light new moral tendencies, without inducing a greater thirst for justice, without stirring the public conscience by latent aspirations' (Durkheim, 1961: 12).

This clarion call to primary teachers that man must go beyond himself to realize his nature, that certain social forms may be insustainable in the light of human needs, is also coupled with an injunction to start with where children are when they leave the family and enter into the second, school-based period of childhood – 'a critical moment in the formation of moral character' (1961: 17). The child must first learn to be attracted to and respect the hand which descends before he can reasonably know when to deflect it. His intellectual and moral life is rudimentary and under-developed and training must carry on, simply, in continuity with the vital but insufficient family base. Teachers must grasp that morality is not something very general but rather it 'is a totality of definite rules ... We do not have to construct these rules at the moment of action by deducing them from some general principles: they already exist, they are ready made, they live and operate around us' (1961: 21). Durkheim is not here making some prototypical denial of the processual 'layeredness' of social life, but is attending to a philosophical point about the 'reality' of the social or moral.

Granted that all human beings are rational and sensate, Durkheim argues that the aim must be to produce in children not 'impatience with all rules, the abhorrence of all discipline ... always abnormal since it prompts us to alienate ourselves from the basic conditions of life' but rather the 'natural' need under normal conditions 'to substitute a new regulation for an old one' ... (1961: 53). All this must be worked in the child who 'has his own nature' which the teacher 'in order to act intelligently upon ... must first of all seek to understand ...' (1961: 129). The child's behaviour is irregular, mobile and marked by tireless curiosity. He wants things to satiety, has no sense of the existence of natural laws, is frequently given to anger (than which there is no passion more exclusive) and excess. We must take the child along the centuries which man has travelled, substituting 'the preference for regular and moderate behaviour for a mind endlessly moving; a veritable kaleidoscope that changes from one moment to the next, emotional behaviour that drives straight ahead to the point of exhaustion'. Our activity must recognize the disposition to habit and suggestibility which are built-in characteristics as well as the fact that the 'child's nature is not so malleable that one can make it take on forms for which it is in no way fitted' (1961: 134).

As we noted earlier, Durkheim's depiction of child nature strikes us as high-flown and dated. Perhaps it is more important to grasp that it is also empirical nonsense and could not have been otherwise. But it is certainly *there*. Durkheim did not see the individual child as tabula rasa, rather it was 'new generations' which he said 'society finds itself so to speak' faced with in this condition (1956: 72 and 125). It was essential that educational practice should follow the child's nature – though again, what this entails practically when he exemplifies it is likely to raise a knowing, late-twentieth-century smile.

Form and content matter

In some respects, though, the deep practicality of his advice has withstood the empirical test of prophecy. The child's openness to even 'the slightest, most vagrant impression' inclined him more to fear the abuse of such power than to be sceptical of the teacher's influence. To ensure 'that education does not make the child a carbon copy of the teacher's shortcomings' we must 'multiply the teachers in order that they may complement one another, and so that the various influences prevent one another from becoming too exclusively preponderant' (1961: 143). The possibility should lie along-side the obvious advantages in every family-grouper's pro-fessional repertoire. Or again, he tells us 'the class is a small society', it has 'its own morality corresponding to its size, the character of its elements and its function'; that ... 'the school-room society is much closer to the society of adults than it is to that of the family', being larger and because its inhabitants are brought together for 'altogether abstract and general reasons', so that its rule 'cannot bend or give with the same flexibility as that of the family in all kinds and combinations of circumstances ... There is already something colder and more impersonal about the obligations imposed by the school: they are now concerned with reason and less with feeling: they require more effort and greater application' (1961: 148–9). He dilates upon the general and practical aspects of authority and punishment – given the aim as 'to inspire in the child a feeling for the dignity of man' (1961: 183) the teacher should ensure that the rule is seen 'to merit the same respect despite the offence committed' (1961: 175). Thoroughly intertwined as egoism ('the subject who says "I" ') and altruism (taking external beings as objects) are in all conscious life, the school must build on the latter. The child's horizons must be extended beyond the organism, to social groups be-yond the family, especially political society. He particularly advocated science in education as Cartesian antidote to over-come the French aversion to the 'too complex to be easily and clearly conceptualized' (1961: 253), a check to abstraction more important than art which, though 'a noble form of play', fails to focus upon reality or life in earnest.

Durkheim's work is full of principled practical curriculum choice. Fauconnet argues that he held that science 'alone teaches us what is grounded in the nature of things – physical nature as well as moral nature – what is ineluctable, what is modifiable, what is normal, what are, then, the limits to effective action to improve nature, physical and moral' (1956: 45). He believed it necessary that contemporary Frenchmen should possess certain non-innate knowledge *categories*, which obtain in the fundamental disciplines. These must be trans-mitted: 'One does not recreate science through one's own

96

personal experience, because it is social and not individual: one learns it ... learning is necessarily implied in the forms constitutive of our understanding. Mathematics, physics, geography, history, language and so on are fundamental areas each with their characteristic contribution, for instance, "duration" from history. The most elementary education must be the most philosophical – the "product" of the cumulative work of generations ... must be transmitted to the child, because it constitutes the very framework of intelligence' (1956: 50–1).

Common base, differentiated outcome

Both form and content, then, are of vital importance. Objectively, education varied with milieux within societies and he saw no justification for this – '... the education of our children should not depend upon the chance of their having been born here or there, of some parents rather than others'. But at the same time, the specialization which 'becomes more advanced daily' in society produces occupations each constituting 'a milieu *sui generis*' which requires particular aptitudes and specialized knowledge, in which certain ideas, certain practices, certain modes of viewing predetermined occupational specialization 'require that in large part the child must be prepared for the function that he will be called upon to fulfil ...' This meant that 'education beyond a certain age, can no longer remain the same for all those to whom it applies' (1956: 68). Its common basis, however, must be the pursuit of society's ideal of man. Here we have the prototypical twentieth-century statement as to the desirability of equality of opportunity (that talent should be able to find its level) on the necessitous basis of common induction. It is a point of great regret, but perhaps of some historic inevitability, that sociologists of education should have concentrated on a social 'class chance' who-goes-to-what-school, narrow conception of equality for most of this century, when Durkheim had laid out a whole agenda of issues so long ago which we are only now entering the spirit of.

In *The Evolution* in particular we have a marvellous intimation of the linkage between historical and contemporaneous forces in education, of the rootedness of the division between the sacred and profane, of the conception of education as the orientation of the whole man, the difference between 'collection' and 'fusion' in curricular terms, of knowledge 'necessity' and human contingency and complexity. Archetype of good structural analysis, it enables us to see form reappear solid beneath substance which, when stirred, gathers transience. Such work always threatens to be impossibly facile or egregiously difficult and Durkheim would undoubtedly disown *some* of the immodest and historically shallow work which has proceeded since under the inspiration of his 'structuralism'. But here certainly is a major source of its inspiration in much of anthropology and sociology.

In educational terms of great relevance to the contemporary 'knowledge' debate, Durkheim's work forces us to face up to the fact that 'man is double ... an individual being which has its foundation in the organism and the circle of whose activities is therefore strictly limited, and a social being which represents the highest reality in the intellectual and moral order that we can know by observations ...' – society (Durkheim, 1968: 16). The implication is clear. Social control and society's existence are joined in the necessity of imposing knowledge categories – both form and substance – upon individuals. Indeed, individuality and change are predicated upon commonality and normality. There can be no difference without similarity, but this does not entail 'subservience' to the cultural. The term itself builds upon a misunderstanding, an inadequacy. Any possibility of apprehending let alone transcending 'the real' depends upon prior input of knowledge. Knowledge forms contain within themselves terms capable of expansion and realignment so as to provide for their own and mutual critique and change. Only men operate them and they operate men. To be acculturated is to be neither freed nor enslaved but rather to be preconditioned for either. It is the general fate of slaves that the form and content of their education shall be oriented towards faith, simplicity and practical accomplishment. Durkheim would remind us that no society as yet has dispensed with their control and that those that suggest that the contrary is instantly possible are merely advocating a switch to their control preferences.

Marx through other mouths

Everybody knows best

There are two real problems in talking about Marx's views on education. First of all, as we have already noted, he hardly expressed any directly; and secondly, after a long period of 'outsideness' in sociological and educational debate Marx is back in with a bang, but also surrounded by the noise of argument as to which of his distinctive periods of work is 'right'. It is an argument complexified by the facts that many of its protagonists say things explicitly upon political rather than traditional scholarly grounds, as well as allowing the rationality of their arguments to implode into the mists of *praxis* – the 'unity' of theory and practice, which is the tenet of practical revolutionaries and 'critical theorists' alike (see Jay, 1974). Praxis is sometimes used in a weakened form of 'acting on principle or in terms of values', even absurdly so at times, so that it is assumed that *all* activity occurs in response to some 'real' belief or interest, directly connected to social position. This is an often half-thought-out reflection of its status as a philosophical concept in Marx. But there is also a more proper sense in which praxis means acting in terms of the inexorable historical process revealed for capitalism by Marx's own researches. In this sense, such action is right before it starts so long as it correctly follows Marx and there is a long run sense in which it is supremely irrelevant on the part of single men, for it must come to pass. Sense one and sense two often inflate one another in a way which explains why some Marxist writing seems so arrogant.

Praxis is one example of the sort of difficulty stemming from the fact of Marx's 'epistemological break' or 'rupture', as described by Althusser, vital if not neat, in 1844; humanist and idealist before, scientific and materialist after. We cannot discuss the 'difference' at any length here, save to say that although Marx worked a long life and modified his ideas (or changed his mind), there is enormous continuity over his creative span. All Western Marxists would assign a central determinative power to the material conditions and relations of production. Some accept what we might call a 'soft' determinist position (man made and capable of reacting, everywhere able to 'create' change), others a much 'harder' view (material conditions are highly determinative, man is a prisoner until he has the key of Marxist understanding with which to penetrate false consciousness and oppression). Yet others seem conveniently able to combine both, ignorant of the stricter contradictions, absolving self-doubt in the claim to 'dialectic' belief, safe in the knowledge that being wrong is the necessary pole of getting it right. As it is difficult, therefore, to categorize Marxist writers for purposes of exposition with any neatness, perhaps we had better begin with the certainty of Althusser.

Education is an ISA

Explicitly eschewing the 'young Marx', Althusser starts with the 'necessity to renew the means of production if production is to be possible' (1971: 123), either simply or on an extended scale. Firstly, this entails reproducing the *material conditions of production* in the sense of raw material, buildings, etc. (involving the well-known 'endless chain' of relations between firms), as well as labour power. Labour power is granted a wage (whose amount has emerged out of the class struggle), so that the worker can reproduce his own power and raise children. But the 'competence' of labour necessary to meet complex socio-technical conditions is provided for more and more outside production, in the capitalist education system.

At school, children learn a number of techniques (like reading and computation) and productively useful elements of literacy and scientific culture, i.e. 'know how'. They 'also learn the "rules" of good behaviour, i.e. the attitude that should be observed by every agent in the division of labour, according to the job he is "destined" for: rules of morality, civic and professional conscience, which actually means rules of respect for the socio-technical division of labour and ultimately the rules of the order established by class domination' (p. 127), i.e. they are subordinated to the ruling ideology which dictates submission for the workers and the reproductive ability to manipulate it correctly for the 'agents of exploitation and repression' (capitalists, managers and 'functionaries').

How the *relations of production* are reproduced is more complex. Marx showed that every society has an economic base (or infrastructure which 'in the last instance' determines the two levels of its superstructure (Law and the State, and the different ideologies). The superstructure has relative autonomy and is capable of reciprocal action with the base. Within it, the State is *repressive apparatus*, enabling class domination and surplus-value extortion. Non-narrowly defined it includes police, courts, prison and army, as well as government and administration. State power may change possession without affecting the State apparatus, e.g. as in *coups d'etat*. The object of the proletarian struggle is to appropriate state power, so as to replace it with its own apparatus.

Althusser wishes to extend Marx's formulation by designating these agencies 'repressive' (RSAs) and adding to them 'ideological' state apparatuses (ISAs) which function 'massively and predominantly by ideology ... *beneath the ruling ideology*' (p. 139), and include religion, education, the family, the law (also an RSA), politics (including parties, trade-unions, mass-communications) and 'culture' in the form of Literature, Arts, Sports, etc. ... No class can stay in power without extending hegemony over these ISAs, and they may be the site of bitter class struggle. They 'largely secure the reproduction specifically of the relations of production, behind a shield provided by the repressive State apparatus' (p. 142).

Under mature capitalist social formations (like the Church in earlier ones), the dominant ISA is education. It takes children when most vulnerable ('squeezed' between it and the family), imparts skills and ruling ideology and ejects the mass at sixteen 'into production', others later into middling technical and white-collar posts. A minority reach the 'summit' to become the agents of exploitation and repression and professional ideologists. Each group is kitted out with suitable ideology as to its function. Other ISAs do similar work but none has children compulsorily for so long. A few teachers are 'heroes' who teach against the system, but most serve to reproduce the vital capitalist elements of 'conscience' and 'freedom' by means of example, through knowledge and literature and by extolling 'liberating' virtues.

School, as with other ISAs, only plays a part in reproducing productive relations: they *are* reproduced in activity by men bearing ideology. The ideology which they bear represents 'not the system of real relations which they live' (p. 155). Despite this 'imaginary distortion', the ideology always insists that ideas do or ought to exist in actions, that it is wrong not to act according to one's ideas, to exercise freedom. Ideologies exist as material practices in an apparatus. Is it school rather than any other apparatus that *does* affect such materiality?

Through Althusser's rather cryptic and highly repetitive prose, we can see that he too sees school as being important, both as to form and content, in the pursuit of its function. In terms of the 'unconsciousness' of ideology we shall see that he has something in common with his contemporary, Bourdieu. He also shares with him a strongly deterministic notion of 'reproduction', even though he formally allows for some play between system-parts. Indeed, we might accuse him of having an 'over-determined' view of system in the same way as Parsons was accused of having such a view of man. Functionalists of the world *do* unite, even if they would not be caught dead in the same conceptual (ideological) chamber, with or without their endogenous variables.

Open Marx

Two outstanding historical Marxist figures remain of relevance to education, Gramsci and Mannheim. Gramsci (along with Lukacs) had provided much of the focus for a general post-war revival in 'humanistic' Marx. In relation to education Gramsci would certainly have agreed with Althusser that schools were among those organizations through which the hegemony of one social group over society was secured. In its nature, that hegemony is obtained by consent – it amounts to 'spontaneous' loyalty of the masses to the dominant group, in virtue of its prestige and 'superior' function. He argues that the effective seizure of power by a new ruling class must be prefaced by a prior victory at the level of cultural and moral pre-eminence in 'civil society'. He held great hope for the expanded humanity of proletarian hegemony, which would flower from its small base of 'organic' intellectuals, who had a vital part to play in propagating and leading cultural and political change. Yet he felt that the traditional forms of education – the scholarship and labour learning – were intrinsic to its nature. Though a degree of conventionality surrounded the contents of intellectuality, and unfair social process certainly determined individual and class access to them, nothing in Gramsci's thinking suggests that his view that 'everyone is an intellectual' means more than that everyone comparatively indulges in cerebral activity. Before or after the revolution, the 'political' and 'civil societies' that made up the superstructure (in a fashion remarkably like Althusser's R and ISAs) would still be manned by 'organic' and 'traditional' intellectuals, so far as we can see. Learning would be no light matter.

Raymond Williams is often referred to as being interested in a Marxist, non-Party, non-physical revolutionary (unlike poor, sweet, stuck Gramsci), English way through the same sort of problems. His erudite and highly readable historical analysis render the nineteenth-century conflict within education as being between democratic, gentling and vocational impulses with industrial interests prevailing, to leave continuingly deep marks upon twentieth-century provision and practice. His work on the relation between educational content and the class system is literary where Mannheim's is philosophical and schematic. Mannheim's vision of how truth might be sustained in a world where men in groups 'developed a particular style of thought in an endless series of responses to certain typical situations characterizing their common position' (Mannheim, 1960: 3), involved an elite in the form of the intelligentsia, sufficiently insulated from class interest and passion. The general questions which he raised about class and group cultures are of great interest and little open work has been done on them. His best remembered distinction lay between general and particular ideology, of a whole age or

103

society on the one hand, and of individual conceptions of truth and error on the other. Mannheim's analysis is impaled on the sharp and unresolved contradiction between a conception of truth independent of knowers and truth as relative to particular ages and classes. Now that we are clearer on some of Mannheim's philosophical muddles (because we know, after Wittgenstein, that forms of knowing are in a sense just different and themselves; and after Habermas that given the ground rules of language, communication 'distorts' in order to let us see, as well as being distorted by power relationships) we may the more usefully be able to utilize his central insights. What they must rule out from our gaze is individually optional truth.

Classroom lib

Change is a wonderful thing, and Marx promises much. So too in recent years have 'phenomenological' approaches which go further than traditional liberalism by insisting on the efficiency of personal renewal. Whitty is dissatisfied with both 'analytic' (phenomenological) and 'possibilitarian' (liberal) stances, particularly the 'premature tendency to celebrate the ecstatic possibilities for freedom which stem from analysing the "varying processes of becoming giveness"' (1975: 115). Reminding us of Marx's dictum concerning the importance of 'real social relationships grounded in the relations of production' (p. 127) as the basis for analysis, he quotes him jointly with Engels as saying that 'all forms and products of consciousness cannot be dissolved by mental criticism ... but only by the practical overthrow of the actual social relations which give rise to this idealistic trickery ... (and) shows that circumstances make men just as men make circumstances' (quoted: p. 127). The necessity is for action in the light of 'the more explicit formulations of the notions of circumstances contained in his (Marx's) later works and those of some of his twentieth-century successors' (p. 128). In good Marxist fashion, knowledge is viewed as an epiphenomenon not of consciousness but other forces, so it is accepted that it is no use trying to wish it away. But there is at the same time a rather incongruous optimism about his enjoining teacher-based research and collaborative learning which celebrates sociability unless they are designed to mask a call to educational entryism.

Freire believes in the power of the word to the point where he believes that to speak a true one 'is to transform the world' (1971: 75). So long as it is authentically (i.e. in the right balance) constituted by 'reflection' and 'action' it is a 'praxis'. 'Dialogue is the encounter between men, mediated by the world, in order to name the world' (p. 76). It is 'an existential necessity', consisting neither in 'consuming' or 'depositing' ideas, 'infused with love', commitment to other men and their liberation, based on faith, hope and processuality. Educating the oppressed, as with taking the revolution to them (for the dialoguers can oppress too) must not be cultural invasion. It must seek out their 'generative themes' which involve 'limit situations' which range from the universal (e.g. freedom and oppression itself), to the 'moment' of more particular tasks, using 'codifications' (sketches, photos, a few words referring to relevant existential situations), for decoding in 'thematic investigation circles' of no more than twenty people, aiming to cover 10 per cent of the population in an area being 'studied'. This leads to 'conscientization', the first step to struggle. 'Culture' is an especially good theme, either with those learning to read or for those enrolled in the post-literacy programme. 'The important thing from the point of view of libertarian education is for men to come to feel like masters of their thinking ...' (p. 118).

Freire gives grounds for his activity, with equal felicity, from thinkers as widely apart as Lenin and Buber, Jaspers and Althusser. There is a sense in which his existentially-rationalized Christianity and Marxism, leaps out from every page and breathes the agony of cultures where schoolteachers with books by Marxist writers were just likely to be taken outside and burned by priest-incited peasants (p. 130). In the land of the starving, the anorexic are kings. Where calories abound they are not well. One might even hope that they were secret eaters. In Freire's own terms 'banking', which appears to apply to all situations where facts or concepts are taught, is pejorative as well as rhetorical when applied to knowledge and learning (which rusts not, neither does it require an object of expenditure). Like the deschoolers – Illich believes that Freire has a 'truly revolutionary pedagogy' – his fame as a possible saviour of western education rests upon extraordinary confusion as to the exigencies of differentiated knowing.

Young also wishes to change students' educational experience, conceding that this may entail our acceptance of 'teachers' struggles as not independent from other struggles in the work places and communities where people live' (1975: 129). Drawing his inspiration from Marxist and existential thinkers like Freire and Greene, he sets in opposition 'curriculum as fact' (a 'commodity-view of knowledge ... rightly criticized as both dehumanizing and mystifying education') and 'curriculum as practice', which does not reduce curriculum reality simply to 'the subjective intentions and actions of teachers and pupils' because this would debar historical understanding and control, but a position where 'no longer can knowledge be viewed almost as private property handed down from the academic discoverers, for the teacher to distribute or "transmit". Knowledge becomes that which is accomplished in the collaborative work of teachers and pupils. Theoretically this has profound implications for existing school hierarchies, and for how we organize educational practice' (p. 133). He underlines that this sort of position does not hinge upon a distinction between 'good–bad teaching' but refers more profoundly to 'assumptions about knowledge as external, to-be-transmitted', which he equates with pupils having a sense of ' "not knowing" at least until his "knowledge" is confirmed by the teacher' (p. 131). He quotes Wittgenstein on the hidden curriculum, Layton on the historical difficulty of insuring relevance in science teaching and teachers everywhere as experiencing the constraint of exam boards and Schools Council. He devotes his own intensive small-scale research (when there is only one thing to know, it is a waste of time looking for a sample to exemplify it in terms of) to the study of pupils' and teachers' meaning in classroom science in the hope, it would appear, of bringing the epistemological house down. This is to be done by neither denying or accepting hierarchies of knowledge as necessary but by trying to 'reformulate them as not in the order of things but as the outcomes of the collective actions of men – and thus understandable and potentially changeable' (p. 135). Or does he? Teachers changing their own classroom practice is not enough; structural limitation on them, within and without school is too sharp and will unhinge their activity. Is the odd law or two of thermodynamics in danger because a collaborative group somewhere have decided not to make entropy one of their Words? Or is Young, in his way, more humbly concerned with the problem that children shall have knowledge more abundantly and relevantly? The latter is the more probable but from the philosophical muddling of his ideas, it is not possible to be sure. Meanwhile we should surely note that the oppositional and questioning quality of his rhetoric has provided inspiration and comfort for those hurt, angry or puzzled by the very real deficiencies of our educational arrangements at personal, knowledge and institutional levels.

The education of girls

A great deal, but certainly not all, of our recent raising of consciousness and practical activity in pursuit of women's equality-liberation has been theorized by Marxist writers. Though not one of them (Jones, 1973) locates the difficulty in respect of education to be at root in the economic structure outside. 'A fundamental paradox underlies any discussion of education for women. On the one hand ... official ideology of equal opportunity for all' stands against the fact that 'options for girls after they have left school are considerably fewer than those open to her male classmates' (p. 114). In consequence, educational experience is differentially valued by boys and girls, girls experiencing a real conflict between educational pressures which, despite obvious institutional biases at the level of provision of some secondary school subjects, is a great deal less sexist than the culture outside. Parents – growingly less so, but still in all classes to a real extent – believe that the education (particularly academic) of girls is less important than that of boys. The performance frontier moves forward. Girls on all measurable counts are more successful until after 11+ and sustain much of their advantage to school leaving (see Dale, R.R., 1974) but have tended to fall off markedly in performance and attendance at A level and onwards, though recent figures show relatively remarkable gains at some of these levels.

Behind all this, of course, lies a family structure where there is a growing degree of convergence of sex roles, but where virtually every empirical study produced on child-rearing and family control still shows (though diminishingly) that we tend to 'bring up' boys and girls differently; that even where grosser sexist manifestations disappear in socialization practices, gentler but ubiquitous pressures direct girls towards greater docility, greater clarity of status orientation within the family. It is not possible here to analyse the social basis of gender differences in any depth. Clearly, parturition and its environs apart, there is virtually nothing under the social sun incapable of achievement. But forces ranging from the deep-seated currents of personality to legal injunction all hedge around male–female differences. Perhaps one had best take one's own guilt on board and point to Ch. 2 which should be read for models of persons but says models of man!

On your Marx

Our consideration of Marxist views here and in the last chapter must leave the impression that Western applications of his thought are many and varied. To many from Marxist societies, some of these views would appear to be hopelessly idealist and playboyish in their tenor, philosophically muddled, having more to do with middle class intellectual coping strategies better analysed by Freud than by the science of historical materialism. What can we say, then, by way of pulling together the central relevance, variously overlooked in unduly hybridized versions, of a Marxist approach to education and social control? It would seem that a viable Marxist view places the question of social control in relation to the power structure and class structure of a society and the formation of social consciousness within them. The mainsprings of formation and change both of structure and consciousness are located in the political and class forces outside of education and at large in society. Education itself is power and class suffused as well as regenerating, in a context where various levels and parts of the social structure are both interdependent and partly autonomous and given therefore both to reaction and inertia. Whereas certainly no Marxist would want to abjure the view that material conditions determine consciousness and social relations in the last instance, modern ones would accord relative autonomy to important parts of the 'superstructure', from the party to the media. Most assign to education a vital but essentially highly passive reproductive function in respect of consciousness, values and tastes, as was indicated in our accounts of Gintis and Althusser and will be revealed when we discuss Bourdieu. The upshot of their deterministic view is in some ways remarkably similar to that of Durkheim and those working in one degree or another in his tradition such as Parsons and Bernstein, whose ideas we shall come to below. If anything, Marxist views are more deterministic, for only possession of the one true faith, even if living, can set their men free. In this view, most traditional concern of sociologists of education with questions of educational access, opportunity, performance and its consequences assume about the same importance as church attendance statistics do to the theologian.

6

Education functions (and Weber lives)

To allocate and select

No one thought it was fair

As every erstwhile sociologist of education knows, Durkheim's inspiration for education lay buried for sixty years and Marx has only just been re-born. The modern sub-discipline came into being to explore the education, economy, class relationship in Weber's world. As he described it, in the first quarter of this century, modern capitalism was characterized by rationality – indeed 'rationality' was a form of domination, of social control. Its spirit, archetypically represented in science, had spread to suffuse the whole of culture and structure. No element, including music, was exempt from it. Its embodiment in human organization came to flower in bureaucracy, differential access was afforded to it by the educational system. The struggle between specialism and cultivation lay behind educational as with all other cultural questions. This struggle conjoined with the democratic tension *vis-à-vis* merit and organization whose focus in the educational system lay in certification.

In an inexplicit way, for sociology of education at the time 'took colouration' rather than 'had a hue', Weber's problems were also those of the post-1945 era. Practitioners at the time would have been most conscious that Weber told them something about 'life chances' (access to economic, political and cultural goods); that Marx's concept of class required expanding to include prestige and party as well as economic (work and market situation) factors; and that chances affected and were affected by education. Access to more or less stylized and specialized curricula meant routes, via 'cultivation' in arts or 'specialization' in science (itself a perversion of the debate), to qualfication (or not) and differential job allocation.

No one laboured under the illusion that the growingly complex educational system was fair or smooth – it simply 'worked' or functioned. Floud and Halsey, introducing their famous *Reader* (with Anderson, 1961), observing that 'the principle of equality of opportunity in education serves an important economic function' asked, 'in the face of this emphasis on innovation and diffusion' what 'becomes of its traditional conservative functions' of value transmission, 'fostering organic solidarity', 'gentling the masses', etc.? The answers in their collection are sketchy. The inevitable fate of school was to select, allocate and acculturate: given what was known of IQ, value, child-rearing practice and language differences at large, the problem of 'talent-wastage' appeared most intractable.

What of the school itself? It is essential to grasp that for a very long time during which evidence was accumulating about 'family background', basic assumptions about the school saw it as important (or a problem), but not so much in its acculturating as in its selective aspects. 'Knowledge' was not a 'problem' except insofar as it was contingently extremely difficult to shoe-horn it into certain heads. But that the right – i.e. 'able to profit' – children should be selected for prolonged exposure to it was of great interest and the focus of much detective work. The limitations of family-background work drove investigators to examine doubts about the shortcomings of 'normal' school operations, especially streaming. This in its turn opened up wider questions of evaluation, content and pedagogy, down to the present corrosive possibilities that knowledge is massively organized 'mystification' and teachers are its class-serving automata.

Organizing folk-norms

The epitomization of the differently unfair modes of educacational selection was offered by Turner. Differing 'organized folk norms', for him, determined 'the accepted mode of upward mobility' through education in England and the United States. Both had open class systems and provided mass education but in England 'elite recruits are chosen by the established elite or their agents and elite status is *given* on the basis of some criterion of supposed merit and cannot be taken by any amount of effort or strategy', as like entry to a club; while in the US 'elite status is the prize in an open contest and is taken by the aspirant's own efforts' (Turner, 1961: 123), the contestants employing a variety of strategies for taking mobility which is not in elite hands to give. These depicted *models* of sponsored and contest mobility systems, respectively, as *organizing norms*, not actual states of affairs, 'guiding ... judgements of what is appropriate or inappropriate in specific matters', highly simplified conceptions of what 'ought to be', which reacted upon objective conditions rather like a Durkheimian 'collective representation'.

Given, then, that they did not encompass existing conditions precisely but rather described a 'strain' towards solving problems in their terms, Turner suggested that under 'sponsorship' there tends to be emphasis on early selection, long training and the right of experts to judge credentials. In 'contest', a wider range of self-acquired capacities including 'material possessions and mass popularity' may be put forward for more popular adjudication. Premature judgements and system-bestowed advantage are feared, whereas under sponsorship, talent may be located for correct development while still pristine and before being overlaid. A history of single (sponsorship) and multiple (contest) elites tended to lie behind the generation of the modes.

From the point of view of social control what matters is that every society needs to maintain 'loyalty to its social system',

112

achieved partly through norms and values, some of which are culture wide, some class specific. 'The most conspicuous control problem is that of ensuring loyalty in the disadvantaged classes toward a system under which they receive less than a proportional share of society's goods' (p. 124). Future orientation, widespread ambition and 'fellow feeling with the elite', kept open until attitudes are firmly established in individuals, combined with a 'delay in clear recognition of realities' until commitment has gone too far for radical change, mark contest mobility. The unambitious are deviants and organized deviance attacks the moral rather than the class system. The US notably avoided class-challenging active revolutionaries. Mystery about the elite, cultivating belief in the superior status and the concomitant lack of competence of the masses to rule, plus early extraction of their 'potential leaders', with matching encouragement of the remainder to 'realistic aspiration', characterized sponsorship. Norms of patronage, courtesy and altruism restrain the elite in such settings. Under contest conditions, insecurity and popular check provide realism, but do not notably engender ethical or altruistic behaviour.

The 'unworthy' may make it in both systems, via 'craft' in contest, and mistaken selection followed by unifying 'cover-up' in sponsored. In sponsored systems, it is strongly expected that those selected will stay the course, more so at higher reaches where contest becomes increasingly specialized. Phantasy aspiration is low and squeezed out early. In contest, education is opportunity for getting ahead *par excellence*, directly vocational in emphasis much earlier on, admixed with 'social adjustment training' as preparation for a world in which the 'rules of intercourse' are absent or unknown. Evidence of the effects of these systems upon personality is limited, Turner argued. He suggested that working class early leaving from grammar school indexed sponsorship's strains (times change ...) while his own research in San Francisco has since added to his doubts that the stereotyped picture of the 'purported working class value system' is not as pervasive or constraining as it is made out under contest. 'Class of orientation' mattered a great deal more than 'class of origin' in his work and details of family background simply did not explain how ambition was

113

generated (Turner, 1964). The application of his approach to British schools by Ford (1969) makes interesting comparison particularly insofar as her limited case-study suggests that a move from tripartism to comprehensive schools tends to reduce social mixing and ossify children's images of the class system.

Turner is in no doubt that mobility actually takes place in terms of *both* modes in every society – his argument is about 'ascendancy' and 'naturalness'. Many of the later empirical attacks upon his formulation seem to have missed this point (e.g. Noel, 1962). It is indeed fascinating to speculate upon the extent to which trends in England and the US have altered the balance since the fifties. For instance, ability grouping tendencies seem to be going in opposite directions with very real growth of 'mixed ability' grouping in British secondaries and 'tracking' in the American high school. Though we have already noted the reality of possible covert selection via catchment areas and 'parental choosing', British tripartism in some degree weakens, or at least a small proportion of British children now attend secondary schools with balanced ability intakes and many go to schools with wider mixes than ever before. Perhaps we might even take, with plenty of caution, the changing fate of the 'tech' (and colleges of further education, as are), as an index and 'safety valve' of the state of the secondary system. Apart from the post-war expansion of craft and technician training, up to degree level, full and part-time, plus new vocational provision for white collar workers, designated colleges have also in some cases effected major expansion into 'O' and 'A' level work. In some measure, this has taken the strain both of the more extreme form of grammar school malcontent (very often middle class by background) and those reacting to the inadequacy of some secondary modern and comprehensive provision. A vital alternative has been available for many young people wanting to continue the pursuit of qualifications but thoroughly 'hung up' with conventional schooling. They have not yet in any sustained way wavered in their willingness to attend our post-Robbins binary system of higher education which, although it has undergone large expansion, has neither departed from an 'ability to profit' criterion or the ethic of 'those who come, get through'. Bewildering though no doubt the range of courses now are in colleges of education, polytechnics and universities for their still mainly straight-from-school aspirants, the system is still fundamentally specialized and elitist in the ability sense, has become the major point of the 'class filter' and still ties the secondary system fundamentally to its nature.

Turner's case, then, in respect of our system, has some resilience. Revived Marxism has made his 'organized folk norms', suitably re-entitled ideologically, quite respectable. We will see below that his 'modes' say something about the same underlying realities as Bernstein's 'codes' of educational transmission and Bourdieu's educational 'habitus'. Both modes and codes rest upon the consent which they are deeply implicated in generating in culture, as well as embedding in identity.

Regulating the temperature

None of this is to say that Turner's conceptions are less than very general or in need of testing out. Hopper has attempted to extend the typology so that it might be applied more widely. He suggests that the selection process might be classified in terms of *how it occurs* (where the degree of centralization and standardization may be measured, and the society's ideology of implementation – how it is to be done – located, e.g. contest or sponsorship); *when it occurs* (as to earliness and degree of specialization of the educational route); and *to whom it occurs, for what reason* (here he distinguishes between different countries' 'ideologies of legitimation' as to who is educationally suitable, 'who' answers differing in terms of universalism–particularism and 'why' answers in terms of collectivism–individualism, both pairs of pattern-variables). All systems have mixed characteristics, the English one, for instance, coming out as having medium centralization and standardization (a lot of local authority/school autonomy combined with 'national' type exams, etc.), high on earliness and degree of specialization of route determination (junior-school streaming, 11+ allocation, differentiated secondary schools, art-science split, etc.), and particularist-collectivistic (which combination Hopper calls 'paternalistic' – 'justified to the population in terms of the society's "need" for people with diffuse skills and certain ascribed characteristics in order that the society might be led by the most suitable people' (Hopper, 1971: 100).

All this may amount to no more than providing extra labels to apply to education, except that Hopper broadens the question out in the context of what he calls the social management of the 'total selection process' (1971: 295), which involves training, selection, recruitment (allocation) and the regulation of ambition. Training includes the inculcation of the social attributes required in upward mobility – teaching 'both through formal and informal means to speak "properly", to use the "correct" accent, to dress "well", to make friends with the "right" kinds of people, etc.' (p. 296), as well as instruction in extrication from present networks and in the exercising of authority. The regulation of ambition is the most difficult part of the task for society, which must scan its talents, encourage children to develop them, get them matched up accurately with more or less difficult tasks and calm the unsuccessful. The problem is a dual one of 'warming up', aspirations–ambitions and then 'cooling out' (the term comes from Goffman via Clark (1961)) those so heated to an appropriateness that matches their station. Mechanisms operating to this end exist at every level of every route through education (their process origins being back again in family and community), both in a local organizational sense and in respect of the long-term goal of adult placement. The 'structural dilemma' represented by balancing these needs is a constant pressure towards conflict and change in education.

Cross-breeding the model: adding transmission

Smith (1973) has broadened out this work to try to provide a model showing how an educational system in an industrial society plays its part 'in a complex series of *distribution processes*' (p. 52) of generations and individuals to social and occupational positions. In particular it provides *selection* – 'the distribution of students among educational routes leading to "qualifications"', and the *transmission* of educational knowledge (including technical and social-skill training, as well as more general 'ways of perceiving' and thinking). It does this in

116

a particular class and occupational context in a society impinging upon it through a pattern of power relations, filtered through ideologically shaped values.

He suggests that an educational system may stand in a *generative* or *derivative* relation to the class system, but usually in a mixture of both. That is, educational institutions may cater for just one class, and confirm its position; or for a mixture of classes, chosen on some other basis, whose future position will depend (in part anyway) on the education that they will have had. The system is controlled by agencies via legal, professional or diffuse *authority* or by manipulating financial or certificatory *resources*. These agencies may be more or less free from one another or subordinated in hierarchical relationship, having authority delegated to them. Their possession of power and the justification for its use will be validated by *ideologies*, which will tend either to favour or oppose change. These will regulate who is chosen and the character of what they are taught, as well as how it is transmitted, over what period and educational routes.

Smith's model sets out to bring together, then, the tradition of work initiated by Turner, and more recent work (e.g. by Bernstein) on the curriculum and pedagogy, to focus both upon who gets channelled where, when, as well as what sort of experience they get *en route*. In this sense it attempts a difficult though laudable and proper synthesis of structural process and knowledge properties.

Ma, they are managing my knowledge

Before Smith had suggested his model, Davies had already castigated any work done 'without a theory of knowledge', for instance of the Hopper type, for above all 'trivializing the cultural content of education' (Davies, 1971: 116). That sort of approach, and those via organizational theory and 'inputs' ('the traditional British approach') and child socialization, are all argued to be deficient in the sense that they do not deal with the 'management of knowledge' as the main intended function of education. In his view a more adequate approach would be to study values, norms and knowledge both at the level of national intellectual styles (in both cultural and structural aspects), and their transmission through educational policies. Davies calls for historical work to see how styles come to dominate, as well as attention to educational power-structure to see how new information is filtered, accepted or rejected. This would very much require the study of knowledge in educational organizational contexts against the background of their 'subcultural inputs'. Such study would concern the generation of knowledge-as-discipline, the control of educational institutions over knowledge imparted and 'the ways in which individuals and collectivities manage the tensions which arise out of the conflict between their own world-view and the discipline-institutional conceptions of knowledge' (p. 130). In his well-chosen words of the song, our study should put us in a position to ask mother to inspect what it is that schooling has done to our cerebration. In terms of the evidence to date, that would be difficult, but the remainder of this chapter and the next, as well as the final one, show what there is.

To structure motivation

Everyone agrees on achievement

While Turner typologized the 'system' in relation to ambition, social control and success, Parsons took the analysis into the school. His initial insight is pure Durkheim (though not the slightest reference is made to him) – while its neatness of fit is pure Parsons. It takes the American elementary school 'class' in a single grade, with one main teacher to be followed by the complex of 'classes' experienced by the pupil at the secondary stage, as its 'unit of analysis'. It faces the dual, inter-related problem of '... how the school class functions to internalize in its pupils both the commitments and capacities for successful performance of future adult roles and ... how it functions to allocate these human resources within the role structure of modern society' (Parsons, 1961: 434). That processes occuring early are vital is clear to Parsons: *ascription* factors like socio-economic status and measured ability begin work from the start to differentiate high-high from low-low children in terms of High school and college-going orientations; *achievement* differentiation in elementary school does its expected work for them, though it is much more problematic for 'cross-pressured' high/low groups, that is, children whose socio-economic status and ability are discrepant.

The child enters school with only his sex-role and predisposition in terms of *independence* level from adults, fundamentally determined. With these, he faces his first 'achieved status' system – he must earn it via performance at teacher's tasks. Schools vary locally but each class is usually about twenty-five in size, taught by a woman. Because schools tend to be neighbourhood in nature, school classes tend to start equal by 'family background', so differentiation by achievement is assured. Teacher systematically evaluates performances on strikingly undifferentiated common tasks. Schools do vary in terms of traditional/progressive and Parsons is not clear whether he believes that these tend to 'match-up' with family background types. The two types will transmit their evaluations differently (more, or less, formally) but in both, teachers' opportunity for particularistic treatment of children is severely limited.

The 'achievements' expected of children are both *cognitive* – writing, maths, etc. ... *and moral* – 'in earlier generations of schooling this was known as deportment, respect for teacher, co-operativeness etc.', 'leading on to a capacity for "leadership" and "initiative" '. The striking fact about elementary grades is that these two elements are *not* clearly differentiated from one another – 'a good pupil is defined in terms of a fusion of the cognitive and moral components ... broadly ... "high achievers" are both the "bright" pupils who catch on easily to their more strictly intellectual tasks, and the more "responsible" pupils, who "behave well" and on whom the teacher "can count" '. Given the general case of elementary school intellectual tasks, the main challenge is to the pupils' 'moral' capacities, a feature which progressivism has lent emphasis to 'suggesting that of the two, it has tended to become the more problematic' (p. 440). Children are differentiated to act in terms of key values, at varying levels of capacity. The transfer of the 'independent' child's identification with parent *to* pleasing teacher, as opposed to the transfer of 'dependent' child's identification with child role *vis-à-vis* parent *to* peer-group, is crucial. It largely presages the college-going split, according to Parsons, with 'independent' children much more likely to sustain the longer educational career.

Teacher is female, but unlike mother is 'universalistic': children must internalize her *role*. Her operations are fundamentally underpinned by the sharing of values between family and school on *the basis of achievement*, including 'above all, recognition that it is fair to give differential rewards for different levels of achievement, so long as there is fair access to opportunity, and fair that these rewards lead on to higher-order opportunities for the successful' (p. 445). But of course with the young child, quasi-motherliness, family and peer group supports temper 'the rigour of the valuational pattern', while the status system which crystalizes in the class, exerts a complicating factor and plays a potentially important part in the creation of the child's independent, family-transcended status. 'Fairness' is the salve of the selective process and concomitant failure, along with status gained from alternative prestige systems. 'Cross-pressured' children are the most greatly affected and, in Parsons's view, much of the so-called 'anti-intellectualism' of American youth attests to 'the *importance* of the selective process through the educational system rather than the opposite' (p. 448).

Parsons's ideas in this article have always been partially masked by the general and somewhat unthinking opprobrium which his ideas have tended to draw down. As is characteristic with many of his analyses, some of the 'continuities' are rather forced. Here for example, the limited and equal nature of what children bring to school, the putative lack of 'achievement' orientation within some families, are deficient. But some of the attacks on his ideas have been simply misconstrued: he never, for instance, argued that family and school were in continuity *except* in relation to the central principle of *achievement* – since become a cornerstone of the new orthodoxy of the 'political economists'. They too seem surprisingly ready to accept the blanket 'contentless capacity' model he outlines and which we shall see developed by Dreeben, below. Meantime,

120

Parsons whose intimations of 'how primary teachers work' were once regarded as offensive in their emphasis upon the 'moral', can now claim to have been prophetic in respect of the emerging flood of classroom interaction studies. The failing he exhibited is of not going far enough in believing how far teachers go in assigning labels.

Schooling, or through the behavioural hoop

Elementary classrooms are places for skills rather than 'subjects', on the cognitive side. Dreeben, explicitly setting out to expand the Parsonian thesis argues that schools have properties unlike other socialization agencies and that in them 'what children learn derive from the nature of their experiences' (Dreeben, 1968: 1). Schools are separate from kin, transitional between families of orientation and procreation, mediate with 'the larger public domain', and specialize in competence production of special kinds on special terms, different from that characterizing preceding home experience. He dwells on moral (confessedly approximate) experiences other than 'traditional symbolic outcomes', that is, those concerned with 'normative outcomes that emerge through pupils' experiences in coping with the sequence of situations whose character is defined by the structural properties of schools'. Given typical school characteristics, these add to psychological repertoire gained in the family 'experiences for learning the distinction between social positions and the persons who occupy them' (p. 21), acquired in an atmosphere of 'in the same boatness'.

Whereas families mix emotional expressivity with day-to-day performance 'the school's *explicit* purpose and *official* reason for existence lie in the area of instruction' (p. 33). Children must be attached to the symbolic and physical expression of performance, especially grades. Playing on pupils' self respect, schools transmit norms (principles of social conduct) as well as cognitive skills and subject matter. Norms are situationally specific, constellational and variably internalized. Those characteristically transmitted in schooling concern independence, achievement, universalism and specificity and are integral to public and occupational life in industrial societies. Individuals typically accept the obligations (unless collabora-

121

tion is called for) to personal responsibility and accountability, perform to general standards and accept judgement by relevant category. Their acceptance or rejection is not just school based, and each norm constitutes a knife-edge, the wrong side of which is incompetence and ineffectualness, helplessness, alienation and isolation.

Despite this latter, undeveloped caveat, Dreeben's picture is altogether too general and idealized. Empirically, one would be pushed to find a school where norms were not actually in the process of being bent, defied or ejected by some. Those more or less pejoratively dealt with by school as an evaluator tend to come to an accommodation more or less angry. It is probably highly true that 'knowledge content' is not the only thing of importance transmitted by school but there is more than Dreeben's account seems to dream of in the state of individual and group interaction in school. Much of the available research work is of very recent origin and we shall refer to it in the final chapter. It will indicate that Dreeben's view, and the curiously similar one of the Marxist 'reproducers', are far too normatively overgeneral to give satisfactory purchase on the complexity of life in classrooms and its purpose beyond. Before we go into that, though, let us look at two particularly penetrating overviews of what school is for. They both context 'school transmission' in a wider setting of general cultural transmission and reproduction, that is, try to link up life within and the society without. They do this without having to shrink their men either to the dimension of eternal puppets in a mystified world or eternal responders without sense of limit, that is to say, their conceptual sophistication in modern sociology is relatively great.

7

Transmission and reproduction: the contemporary work of Bernstein and Bourdieu

Bernstein: change within limits

Basic dichotomies

As well as having produced work which is highly pertinent to our theme, Bernstein and Bourdieu stand apart at the moment as sociologists of education who move regularly between the hard taskmaker of empirical research and the relatively compliant maid of theorizing. Moreover, their theorizing is in rather the grand manner, attempting to link structural, cultural, institutional and individual levels with concepts of some generality which perforce only in part have (or can be) subject to evidential test. They have for some time known one another's work well and have both written explicitly in reflection upon their intellectual progress. They are therefore maximally available to our inspection.

Bernstein is a self-avowed Durkheimian: 'I have yet to find *any* social theorist whose ideas are such a source (at least to me) of understanding of what the term *social* entails' (Bernstein, 1975: 17). He has over the course of his work sought to force the Durkheimian mode into public issue, but his thinking is inevitably open to and influenced by other sources as well – most obviously Marx and Mead. His work on education which is mainly conceptual rather than empirical is very much of a piece with, and runs parallel to, his work on sociolinguistics, which is both. All his work is deeply concerned with analysis of changes in forms of social control and their connection with the class structure. Bernstein claims that his most important starting point is Durkheim's *Division of Labour*.

That much of his writing on education takes the form of using a number of basic Durkheimian categories – mechanical and organic, closed and open, content and form, sacred and profane – is certainly the case. In his earliest educational papers he expressed his analysis of the secondary school in terms of the ideas of 'expressive' and 'instrumental orders' – 'two distinct, but in practice interrelated, complexes of behaviour which the school is transmitting to the pupil: that part concerned with character training and that part which is concerned with more formal learning' (p. 38). The former sprang from the school's image of 'conduct, character and manner', the latter from the exigencies of 'facts, procedures, practices and judgements necessary for the acquisition of specific skills'. A child's involvement in either might be strong or weak, varying with his family's understanding and acceptance of their respective ends and means, his psychology, and the ongoing experience of school. It might vary from commitment to alienation, and its meaning would tend to depend upon his class. The school, by its choice of organizational emphasis, could alter pupils' role involvements.

This brief allusion misses the real strength of the paper, which was its capacity to make sense of the variety of routes whereby pupils reached their role involvement. It marked a quite decisive complexification of bloodless class stereotypes. For instance, it made serious educational sense of the 'detached' working class pupil, bright, instrumentally involved, willing to go through the motions, in some degree, of the expressive order, but either from taste or concern about wider social relations, unwilling to accept its ends as well. It also made real the 'estranged' middle class child, understanding the

124

instrumental ends and accepting them, but unable to manage the means. Having a grasp upon real events, it put real cases where only class puppets had been (and still frequently are).

In his work on ritual, Bernstein spelt out some of the structure-process dimensions of his 'orders' more fully. He depicted the forms of relation which controlled instrumental and expressive transmissions as bureaucratic, or not. Under certain conditions, he argued, the expressive order was prone to either extensive consensual or differentiating ritualization, both 'major mechanisms for internalizing and revivifying the social order', maintaining 'continuity, boundary ... ambivalence ...' (p. 50). Consensual rituals (ceremonies, dress, etc.) took away the child from outside membership and into the school, differentiating ones (marking off groups within) assigned and confirmed his place in it.

The degree of expressive ritualization was likely to vary in relation to whether pupils were grouped on the basis of some fixed or non-fixed attribute. The former produced stratification, with ritual communicated in a 'verbally both highly condensed and ... redundant' way, the latter, differentiated, with an expressive order communicated in a more verbally elaborated and manipulated way, social control being individualized and therapeutic (p. 62). Differential treatment, say of exam and non-exam children, along these lines was an evident possibility even within the same school.

The theme of the incursion of social, ideological and occupational change and schools' response to them, is constant and became most widely popularized in *Open Schools – Open Society?* where Durkheim's concepts of mechanical and organic solidarity are applied with great metaphorical vigour (in literal terms they are used quite misleadingly) to the analysis of schools moving from traditionalism to progressivism – from closure to openness. The exciting new element drawn into the discussion is Douglas's conception of purity and mixing of categories. This is clarified and adapted in the concept of 'boundary' in Bernstein's analysis of educational knowledge, which is discussed below.

Bernstein wanted concepts that 'could be used at the level of classroom encounter, at the level of codes, and as a means of broadly characterizing transmission in different societies'. They had to be able to 'hold together ... structural and inter-actional levels in such a way that change could be initiated at either level ... allow for responsiveness and change in structure' but also 'indicate that there was at any one time a limit to negotiation' (1975: 9). They should apply to a range of transmission agencies (family, school, etc.) and be able to show how changes in the sources and their social basis had 'significance for the shaping of mental structures'. Clearly, any conceptual kit capable of spanning this range was bound to have enormous generality. The problem was, could it also have the sensitivity which led to empirical testing? Bernstein's own answer is 'yes' – he found concepts which transcend his earlier work on family types and control, as well as some measure of his sociolinguistic work.

What are the ideas? They are concepts used to analyse the 'three message systems: curriculum, pedagogy and evaluation ... through which formal educational knowledge can be considered to be realized' (p. 85). Valid forms of content, its transmission and realization on the part of the taught are underlined by 'codes' or social principles as to *classification* and *framing*, both of which refer to boundaries. 'Classification refers to the nature of the differentiation between contents in the message system, curriculum', while 'frame is used to determine the structure of the message system, pedagogy', referring 'to the form of the *context* in which knowledge is transmitted and received' and 'the strength of the boundary between what may ... and ... may not be transmitted in the pedagogical relationship ...'. It 'refers to the range of options available to teacher and taught in the *control* of what is transmitted and received', as to selection, organization, pacing and timing (pp. 88–9). Framing also refers to the relationships of school and non-school knowledge. The remaining 'message system, evaluation, is a function of the strength of classification and frames' (p. 89). These can vary independently of one another.

The analysis does not refer to *what* is classified (in this sense, it is in the 'contentless' tradition or put another way, it can handle any content) but it can cope with internal power and identity components. Bernstein exemplifies it through the erection of a typology of educational knowledge codes with strong classification producing a collection code (with subtypes); and marked reduction in classification, an integrated code, varying in terms of strength of frames. Collection codes may be specialized (pure or impure) or non-specialized, subject-based or course-based. Integrated codes refer 'minimally to the *subordination* of previously integrated subjects *or* courses to some *relational* idea, which blurs the boundaries between subjects' (p. 93). It is either teacher- or teachers-based, the latter subdividing into subject- or subjects-. Framing may vary as with collection codes, though obviously more so.

Vitally, 'principles of power and social control are realized through educational knowledge codes and, through the codes, enter into and shape consciousness' (p. 94). For instance, hypothetically in the English version of the European collection code (i.e. with *exceptionally* strong classification, but relatively weaker framing), 'a membership category is established early in an educational career, in terms of an early choice between the pure and the applied, between the sciences and the arts, between having and not having a specific educational identity. A particular status in a given collection is made clear by streaming and/or a delicate system of grading. One nearly always knows the social significance of where one is and, in particular *who* one is with each advance in the educational career' (p. 95). Self-perpetuating subject loyalty is developed; the process starts early whereby pupils/students become increasingly *different* as they become older, producing clear cut, bounded, pure educational identity. Switching requires resocializing, subject loyalty producing a 'sense of the sacred', the 'otherness of educational knowledge' and resistance to code change. Its deep structure is '*strong boundary maintenance creating control from within through the formation of specific identities*' (p. 96).

The 'profane' aspect of knowledge resides in its property

aspect and children are early socialized into its privacy and their possession of it. The framing of such a collection code is arranged in such a way that the 'ultimate mystery' of the subject is revealed very late in the educational life and then only to a few who '*experience* in their bones the notion that knowledge is permeable, that is orderings are provisional, that the dialectic of knowledge is closure and openness' (p. 97). For the many, socialization into knowledge is socialization into order, impermeability, alienation. Collection code frames screen out everyday knowledge early on, a principle weakened only for control of the less able or other educational 'deviants' who believe, or have believed of them, that 'uncommonsense' educational knowledge is inappropriate.

Change in such an English context is very difficult, and organizational style can change without code alteration. Change, however, is in a sense presupposed in respect of integration codes. Here contents are subordinated to a relational idea, pedagogy and evaluation tend towards a common style and increase pupil-, while reducing teacher-discretion. Pedagogy '*is likely to proceed from the deep structure to the surface structure*' (p. 102), emphasis will be on ways of knowing rather than states of knowledge, the theory of learning will tend to be one of group- or self-regulation.

Visible and invisible pedagogies

Bernstein expands substantially upon the origins and nature of weak classification, weak frame educational transmission in his latest paper on visible pedagogies, where 'general problems of control and ... *class related* modalities of control' (p. 14) are more closely linked. Impetus towards this further analysis sprung, among other sources, from concern about the classificatory origin of symbolic property in general and the idea that 'behind weak classification is strong classification' (p. 14), and in particular, its bearing upon the use of weak classification and frames for working class children in primary school.

This 'invisible pedagogy' at the infant/pre-school levels is characterized in terms of implicit teacher control, emphasis on context arrangement within which the child has wide discretion as to his work, movement and social relationships, de-emphasis on specific skill transmission/acquisition, and diffuse and multiple evaluatory criteria. It differs from 'visible' basically 'in the *manner* in which criteria are transmitted and in the degree of specificity of the criteria' (p. 116).

In invisible pedagogy classrooms, the child's (inner) readiness and (outer) busyness will have high salience for the teacher to whom play is central. Through play, the child 'exteriorizes' – makes himself available – to teacher, who may filter his spontaneity through her principled surveillance. Stimuli – more or less palpable – are presented to him so that he may make his own unique marks in personalized action. Betraying its class origins, 'play is work and work is play' (p. 118) in this orientation.

The 'theology of the infant school' is compounded from, predominantly, Piaget, Freud, Chomsky, ethology and Gestalt. It tends to devalue sequence, see learning as tacit and invisible, abstract biography, see adult socializers as dangerous and hold theories which 'can be seen as interrupters of cultural reproduction', and are therefore viewable as progressive/revolutionary. The child is facilitated and accommodates; imposition and domination go.

The key question becomes what is invisible pedagogy interrupting? Bernstein's argument is that its introduction first took place in the private educational sector for a 'fraction' of the 'new' middle class – i.e. 'those who are the new agents of symbolic control' (p. 136), major and minor professionals concerned with the servicing of persons. Their ideology of education, as opposed to the strong classifications and frames of the old middle class, are now firmly institutionalized in the infant school. This new middle class arises out of 'increases in the complexity of the division of labour of cultural or symbolic control', which it has appropriated. It is marked by *personalized* organic solidarity in family socialization, based on weak classifications and frames, in distinction to the 'old' which is marked by *individualized* organic solidarity based on strong classification and frames in family and home. 'The new middle class is an interrupter system, clearly not of class relationships, but of the *form* of their reproduction' (p. 121), signalizing in Bourdieu's terms a change in *habitus*, not function. Their drive is towards the socialization of their young as *persons* rather than *individuals*, ambiguous in identity, flexible in role performances, socialized to encourage visibility and manifest uniqueness in the service of cultural interruption which ensures their place. As their position is contradictory, they must find their way to the restricted positions of superiority in the class structure via variety, expression and interpersonal skill. They will tend to want visible secondary school pedagogies for their children to consolidate what the primary school has 'located' and opened up. Indeed the invisible pedagogy presupposes a long educational life.

Its further presuppositions are, in Bernstein's terms, a middle-class conception of time and space, an elaborated code of communication oriented towards relatively context-independent meanings, a small class of pupils and 'a middle-class mother who is an agent of cultural reproduction' (p. 125). 'The mother' is described in relation to her 'old middle class', but not her 'working class', counterpart. Weak classification and frames anchor her to her children, 'surveillance is totally demanding', but 'her own socialization into both personal and occupational identity points her away from the family' (p. 125). She seeks the pre-school with congenial ambience for her child.

This delineation of mother appears to be far too firmly class-limited except possibly in respect of 'occupational identity', where the 'working-class' mother tends to work for money rather than more symbolic reward. 'Person orientation' in socialization is certainly far from being an exclusively 'new middle class' phenomenon, even if as a group they first took out the patent. In the most important sense, of course, these are matters requiring empirical clarification rather than conceptual quibble. Meanwhile Bernstein can claim the new group's uniqueness in terms of their 'sharp and penetrating contradiction between a subjective personal identity and an objective privitized identity' in terms of socialization (p. 126); and we can assume that this is not just applicable to this class fraction.

In terms of the working-class child, Bernstein's claim is that weak classification and framing in school render his family and community culture capable of inclusion in classroom experience, hence 'the invisible pedagogy carries a beneficial potential' for him (p. 127). However, he suggests, it is the nature of and the relations inherent in visible pedagogy which are more understandable to working-class parents. Well understood, cumulative competencies go with the introduction of invisible pedagogy. Forms of social control may be at variance between home and school and the new theory may regard mother's help as irrelevant or harmful. Mother may need resocializing or ignoring in its terms. If so, home-school power relations will be disturbed, and this may react within the home where forms of control may be less explicit. Powerful teacher and deeply suspicious mother may well be the confrontation produced. Again, only empirical study will show how far these class hypotheses are upheld. Whatever else the world of relationships between parents and schools is at the moment, it is far from neat, and growingly less easily stereotyped, not least because the additional problems created by the newness of 'invisible' practices are countervailed to some extent by the extra permeability of these schools to parental presence and information seeking.

Bernstein would argue, though, that the evaluatory information available is quite different under visible and invisible modes, and suggests that cut-off working-class parents 'are forced to accept what the teacher counts as progress' (p. 131). No doubt a middle-class parent or two could also attest to the relative feeling of powerlessness at this point. We have here an extremely complex area of power negotiation, centring around the labelling and meaning of child attributes by and to teachers and parents. Part of the outcome (in class terms) may also be part of the process (via the 'class meanings' assigned by teacher, parent and child). Bernstein sees invisible pedagogy increasing teachers' evaluatory power, both in covert and overt forms, over the child who is often an 'innovatory message' (frequently welcomed?) *vis-à-vis* the home. He also suggests that classroom situations are likely to prove most complex upon empirical examination – 'we shall find to different degrees a stress on the transmission of *specific* isolated competencies' (p. 132), entailing a hidden (invisible pedagogy)

131

curriculum of strong classification with weak frames!

Finally, Bernstein makes a series of observations about discontinuities in pedagogical types between educational institutions and the world of work. Work can either be *excluded* or *fit* with education in class societies, but they 'cannot be integrated at the level of principles'. However, weak classifications and frames have the potential for 'greater ambiguity but less disguise' and hence 'the potential for making visible social contradictions' (p. 135). In the spirit of one of his more pungent analogies, we might say that behind every collapsing toilet-roll holder, there may hide the future squatter's rent-book.

Is anything mightier than the code?

The empirical work called for by Bernstein to evaluate these hypotheses is partly but necessarily slowly under way under his own and other auspices. There are relevant pieces of cognate work already available, for example that by Sharp and Green (1975) as we shall see below. The span of work that would be required merely to illumine the range of the class-pedagogy ideas is staggering. It would need to encompass careful historiography in terms of the changing class system, as well as long-term studies of the effect of schooling on identity and performance from the pre-school on, as well as more limited work in school and classroom. This is the fate of any conception of any scale or complexity. Bernstein's work entails both. It is a picture of light and shade, of necessity and freedom, change within limits. He lets it go, conceptually, with a reluctance which sometimes agonizes the prose as it betokens an anxiety over the creative-approximate power of categories. One is inclined not to quibble about some of the fine print in which the news is (at times irritatingly) set but rather to go out oneself and make some, by rejoinder and test. His major working categories, like classification and frame, are in their nature immensely formal and in need of exemplification and the concomitant modification which goes with the vitality of real-world test. In the pessimistic and over-ideological educational debate of the last decade, Bernstein has been accused of sins ranging from hypostasizing social class and knowledge disciplines, to 'inventing' cultural deprivation and 'pushing' integrated codes. Leaving aside those complaints made in error or envy, what most omit is that Bernstein's conceptual scheme, like that of Durkheim which informs it, has enormous tensions within it. It assumes the primacy of the social and the non-individual facticity of knowledge. It presupposes that explanation itself rests upon adequate conceptual hierarchy. But it admits no Messiah. Particular class, economic and cultural systems may be fed through it for analysis of their relations. When the last curtain is parted, what will be revealed is another specific code, eliciting, generalizing and reinforcing those relationships necessary for its continuance.

Bourdieu: plus ça change ...

Structured structure

Of all the people whose work is of direct relevance to our theme of education and social change, Bourdieu is the most self-announcing and self-placing. He is both a structuralist (in a long, mainly anthropological tradition from Durkheim on) and a Marxist wishing 'to go beyond the conflict between these two traditions, though what we have learned from the analysis of structures of symbolic systems (particularly language and myth) so as to arrive at the basic principle behind the efficacy of symbols, that is the structured structure which confers upon symbolic systems their structuring power' (1971: 1255). Symbolic systems, in their nature, provide both meaning and a consensus on meaning. Those that make up the 'structured structure' or ruling culture, include within themselves in transfigured form the 'structure of prevalent socio-economic relationships ... which are consequently perceived as natural, so contributing to the symbolic buttressing of the existing balance of forces ... In short, culture classifies – and classifies the classifiers.' Enter the Chinese box, Parisian style, to the world transfixed by definition.

Its nature is determined directly by Bourdieu's choice (heritage?) in terms of the 'cultural unconscious', which affects him as all other thinkers. His own 'conscious intellectual choices' which are always directed by his own culture and taste, which are themselves interiorizations of the objective culture of a particular society, age or class (1968: 180) (now you choose it, now you don't), stem pre-eminently from the conjunction of Durkheim and Marx ('today's structure, unconscious and praxis'). This conjunction can be thoroughly mutually supportive in a view of reality as intellectual and linguistic patterns transmitted, plus the pattern's pattern. To fight it would be a dangerous practice, for a French man of letters, that we would no doubt call *habitus interruptus*. Wise men ask not where lies the real to which they refer, but rather get on with the belonging: 'mediate, knowing acquisition will always differ from an immediate familiarity with the native culture, in the same way as the interiorized subconscious culture of the native differs from the objectified culture reconstructed by the ethnologist' (1967: 206). This theoretical combination allows him to make exciting observations on a whole range of questions about structure, culture, identity and their relation to education. But it also seems to leave his analysis in a highly static and overdetermined state – a sort of cumulation of the inevitability of Marx and Durkheim, without their dynamic. The cooking, however, is distinctly French, and no one should complain that one meal does not equal nutrition.

Cultural capital, habitus and education

We may indeed take 'taste' as the starting point of Bourdieu's analysis. Culture distinguishes between the things worthy of speech and thought and those not. Taste, broadly defined, is competence at deciphering the extrinsic clue to the 'thinkable' among cultural objects and the attitude to be adopted to them. This has to be set against the background of repressive society (or 'social formation'), which at a given point in time will have a given class structure. Cultural capital 'comparable to economic capital, transmitted by inheritance and invested in order to be cultivated ...' (Kennett, 1973: 238, quoting *La Reproduction*), circulates within its space. Each class has its culture whose contents are 'arbitrary'. The relations of the classes are, of course, unequal. In particular, the access of the dominant groups to 'symbolic violence', i.e. power which succeeds in imposing meanings as alone legitimate, while dissimulating in regard to its own base, is extremely unequal.

It is also self-confirming. Symbolic relations are both dependent upon and autonomous from relations of force. This would explain, for instance, why any given sociological theory *might* come to be defined as *the* principle of sociological knowledge and, at the same time, why the theories of Marx, Durkheim and Weber relate to *their* social basis in a system of power relations, and why they produced *those* theories to the exclusion of others.

School, far from being a liberating force and a means of mobility 'is in fact one of the most effective means of perpetuating the existing social pattern' (Bourdieu, 1966: 32), treating social inequalities and cultural heritage as natural phenomena. It becomes increasingly important as a form of domination in an age growingly suspicious of naked imposition. It is not, though, alone in this respect. 'Habitus' is the durable formation of social genetic capital – 'the intellectual, moral and aesthetic mode of integration of a social group' (Kennett, 1973: 242), and is mainly acquired during socialization. Group members bring it – including language – as a more or less appropriate 'stock' or 'style' to school. The importance of its intangible dimension is never more revealed than at examinations, particularly of a high academic order, where sociologists using suitable non-mechanical ways of collecting data can reveal the importance of such imponderabilia.

In short, it is possible to show a 'law governing the process of differential elimination' (Bourdieu and de Saint-Martin, 1970: 345) in the competitive French scholastic system. At each stage, surviving groups are demographically, socially, scholastically and 'secondarily' more different than the group as a whole. The further up the stages one goes, the more important certain school and background (in status and cultural capital terms) privileges become. Successful working-class children among the ablest French secondary school pupils come from quite disproportionately cultured and 'qualified' homes.

The psychic approbation received by 'survivors' like themselves leads them to reject the 'virtues which have helped them gain their success in favour of the ideological representation of scholastic success' (ibid., p. 345) which are a part of the upper-class habitus. This clears the way to locating the cause of failure (or success) in natural inequalities, and legitimates the peculiar French emphasis on scholastic precocity as a virtue. Social privilege is thus ideologically transformed to natural privilege; social capital is transferable into scholastic capital.

Dependence by means of independence

Here as everywhere in Bourdieu's scheme of things, particular values – in this case scholastic – and the values of the dominant classes, are in harmony. The relationship of education and class is one of 'dependence by means of independence'. The apparent devotion of the educational system to scholastic virtues (its *autonomy*), masks the fact that 'the systems of manners distinguished by scholastic taxonomies always refer (with whatever degree of refinement) to social differences, because in cultural matters the manner of acquisition is perpetuated in what is acquired in the form of a certain way of using the acquisition' (its *subservience* to the class system) (p. 354). This is evidenced by the traditional pecking order among subjects (French and maths demand talent and gifts, geography, natural science, etc. work and study), which acts selectively upon class of students: lower-class swots and upper-class habitus bearers choose as expected. The legitimacy of the literacy elite and its predominantly upper-class background is perpetuated. The disparagement of the pedantic and the glorification of the gifted mask the selective reality of the examinations.

What is true among the 'abler' and higher reaches of the French system has its counterpart below. Parents and children internalize as hopes the objective chances of mobility and these condition their attitudes to school, 'and it is precisely these attitudes which are most important in defining the chances of success in education, of accepting the values and norms of the school and of succeeding within the framework and thus rising in society' (1966: 34). The 'class ethos' so developed combines with cultural capital to determine in-school behaviour and attitudes and differential elimination.

The school has its expectations of what children of various sorts normally achieve. It provides its side of the process both via its characteristic pedagogies and language uses, as well as teachers' inclinations to 'transmit an aristocratic culture' – unconsciously inevitable in Bourdieu's view. 'It is quite clear that such a process can only work perfectly as long as it can recruit and select students capable of satisfying its objective demands', that is 'individuals possessing a cultural capital (and able to make it pay off) which it presupposes and endorses without openly demanding it or transmitting it methodically' (Bourdieu, 1966: 41). 'Mass education' is its opposite, and education cannot meet it from within its own conservative resources. At the moment, it copes by responding to new ranges of children within it who 'take refuge in a kind of negative withdrawal which upsets teachers, and is expressed in forms of disorder previously unknown', with a policy which lets matters take their own course to bring crude social handicaps into play and for everything to return to normal' (pp. 41–2). 'Widespread compensation' would be required to really begin to liberate the eliminated. As it is, the 'system can help to perpetuate cultural privileges without those who are privileged having to use it' by its endorsement of inequality. Society, in Weber's terms, allows social class monopoly of education – 'a monopoly of cultural goods and the institutional signs of cultural salvation' (p. 43), in a rigid way. Bourdieu is sceptical of the social costs and conditions of high degrees of mobility even having been fully considered, let alone being in danger of coming to pass. Meanwhile, 'the controlled mobility of a limited category of individuals, carefully selected and modified by and for individual ascent is not incompatible with the permanence of structures' (Bourdieu, 1973: 71) – indeed it stablizes and perpetuates them.

Taking us out of ourselves ... or in?

Bourdieu presents us with an interesting range of considerations. The analysis of a different culture offers insight upon what we take for granted in our own. Even when he refers to areas which we think that we know well, it is salutary to be

137

reminded of the margin between the wish and the fact – for instance, of the way in which the *creation* of class-attitudes and expectations *of* school *by* school was actually revealed by Plowden in its National Survey but conceptually 'suppressed' at the same time by overlay with 'attitude' factors (Bernstein and Davies, 1969). Bourdieu's work also, from our point of view, has the virtue of concentrating on the successful and the privileged, groups notably neglected in the British and American literature. His theoretical eclecticism is refreshing and, in the end, perhaps his analysis shows the rather static perfection of educational and cultural reproduction *because* the contemporary French conditions which it analyses have these qualities. As with Bernstein, we lack the historical dimension in his work which would enable us to see how it came to be like that, except insofar as we can infer that a general Marxist account would apply.

We can also infer from his work on 'intellectual fields' that there is *some* competition for cultural legitimacy: 'Any cultural act, whether creation or consumption, contains the implicit statement of the right to express oneself legitimately' (1968: 175), within the structure of the intellectual field. Cultural works are more or less consecrated – Bach more than Brubeck more than cake-baking – but parts of the intellectual field are not equally interdependent, there is some 'play'. However, as Kennett points out, the powers-that-be in Bourdieu seem always likely to win. For example, even the writer's product is adapted to fit the nature of social reality.

But this, in the nature of structuralist analysis *is* the strength of the reminder that in *change* there is always *même chose*. It is also the quality that disables structuralism from more than agnosticism about ontological ('really real') questions. Bourdieu does *not* 'de-reify' knowledge, he simply asserts that its basis is arbitrary and then goes on to tell us how it is extremely concretely reproduced in class interests. He puts away the problem of the very real basis of his own knowledge in Durkheim and Marx by simply assigning it to a tradition (we are all, this analysis *is*, in a tradition), which entails its 'arbitrariness' too. Bourdieu's 'structuralism', like anyone else's is a pattern locator. Which patterns are looked for and what sense is made of them depends upon the substantive form of discourse which 'fleshes out' the structuralists' intentions. Of Bourdieu we might ask, whence his 'arbitraries'? There is nothing in him which constitutes a view of reality seeking 'to benefit more than a powerful few' (Kennett, 1973), but it is an extremely cultured way of crying 'Help!' in the face of an over-determined vision.

8

Inside schools and classrooms

School as a containable adjuster

We have already looked at a good deal of history and conceptual speculation as to what goes on in school. But what is school really like? In terms of sociological research we know a bit about some aspects of school organizations, less about classrooms and almost nothing about content and teaching methods as they relate to individual children's educational identity. As school *is* teachers and subjects and classrooms, in the main, to children, this is a bit unfortunate for our enterprise, no matter how neatly we get our conceptions of schooling to fit in with our conceptions of the class, economic and political systems.

What can organizational analysis do?

As organizations, schools have never been terribly widely studied (for summaries, see Davies, 1973b; Musgrove, 1973). This may well be because they have not been regarded as particularly complex or problematic in this respect. Organizations which are in private ownership and/or which have obvious production goals have received much more attention, a great deal of it paid for by owners who wish to cut costs and improve efficiency. There is quite a rich and varied body of evidence on industrial organizations dating back as far as to Taylor's 'efficiency era', exploring goals, bureaucracy, management techniques and communications, human relations, decision-making structures and technology. A lot of it is marred by 'managerialism' (which has its parallel in education), which means usually that it has been assumed that the organization's main sociological purpose is the same as its owner's or manager's explicit goals (which would be like accepting that a school was 'about' what its headmaster or the education officer said it was about). 'Systems' approaches have also been over-employed – they are especially appealing when you are quite sure that you know what is 'best' or normal for the organization (for instance, like making a profit or a revolution, or as with Richardson (1973), Freudian openness of adjustment). There is everything to be said sociologically – despite the fact that organizations are usually explicit, rational creations set up by known people to aim at announced ends – for treating them as 'for' as many things, 'for' as many people, as they 'do', in the first instance.

The best ideas from traditional organizational approaches would still be well worth applying to schools at all levels, from their 'management', down to their 'politics' among both staff and students; and their 'technology' and 'human relations', both as embodied in overall curricular and grouping practices, and as daily exemplified in teaching, learning and other activity in classrooms.

What we haven't got

But at the same time, it is clear that schools are quite *distinctive* organizations – they are publicly accountable, people and knowledge negotiating and processing, compulsory, 'improving' institutions. They carry within themselves a quite unique combination of tensions in terms of the contradictions or paradoxes which society requires them to bear. Most of these have emerged, in effect, in earlier chapters, but we must now polarize the most vital of them, for it also helps to explain the

141

relative lack of sociological research evidence on schools and the part which they play in social control.

The ideal of educational theory and practice is almost universally to produce the 'best' from each educand and to imbue him or her with a sense of the worthiness of their own maximized efforts. The ideal, alas, celebrates an institution manned by saints, attended by sweet innocence, preparing for a world where all hierarchies are adequate or none exist. Even in more temperate terms, education is supposed to do you good and educational institutions and their masters cannot easily confess that they do contingent, let alone pre-planned 'bad'. Some failure is occasioned by resource inadequacy, whether of hardware, 'places' or person-attributes. But much of it is inherent in the nature of the modern enterprise. Schools 'cool out', schools prepare children 'for failure', schools withhold knowledge, physical and time resources, in terms of the ideal, the aspirations of their users and society's prestige systems, *as well as all of their converses*. Schools *are* in Bernstein's terms 'repeater systems' via their curricular, pedagogical, grouping, etc. messages. In the 'public funds' atmosphere of financing state education, one of the things which constantly tends to be overlooked is that altered pedagogy – for instance, the introduction of 'interrupting' invisible pedagogy – entails quite different (from that which it replaces) cost and economic resource considerations for its successful institutionalization. Even more fundamentally, the school system which successfully universalized the production of nothing but 'difference' would be a contradiction in terms on the basis of 'thinkable' social conditions. Schools are reproducers of normalcy. They are containable adjusters. They are this in all known societies.

That this is the case, neither constitutes an argument for deschooling (for complex societies without schools might be badder), nor for declaring the universal brotherhood of all knowledge (of the Subanum and the Sorbonne, or the 'common'- and 'uncommon'-sensical), in the interests of abolishing invidious difference (holding nothing back has its own special terror). But it does help us to understand the resistance of educational systems to certain sorts of probing and exposure, and their inability, in any given nexus of relation-

142

ships within the system, to effect certain sorts of change. It also makes clearer the terms upon which certain sorts of investigatory work would have to be done, as well as the possible prurience of some of its protagonists. As with sex, race and the powers of the police, the theology of schooling is living – though there appears to be little in camp, colour or cell that has not been subject to recent searching investigation.

It is as well then to see what sort of studies we have not got, by and large, of schools. We know nothing very much about adult relations in schools, that is to say, about the actual formal or informal processes of influencing and deciding that inform curricular, grouping, timetabling, manpower allocation, etc. arrangements; even less about these decisions at the local authority level. Esland's work suggests the importance of knowing about teachers, though enthusiasm for and misunderstanding of the nature of 'paradigms' produces a rather limited and moralized aspect in his discussion (Esland *et al.*, 1972). There is plenty of bloodless work upon teacher characteristics and 'professionalism', some of it chasing the rainbow of schools as 'bureaucracies', but this is hardly what is wanted by way of information as to how school is teacher 'shaped'. This is not to say that biographical and career information on teachers is useless or that schools do not have bureaucratic elements or characteristics but rather to express a preference for analysing teachers doing jobs on sites which are a thoroughgoing mix of the routine (and bureaucratizable) and nonroutine.

The evaluation and administration of allocation policies at lay and professional levels in LEAs, how parents actually relate to schools (not the idealized nonsense of 'home-school relations'), how many truants, how 11 + transfers are done, etc., etc. – are all largely areas of un-knowledge. They pall in comparison, of course, with questions of how words and deeds in the classroom pass by or get into pupils heads, leaving not only knowledge (quite a lot known about the intended, testable type), but also attitude, altered self-concept, view of the world, and so on (about which we know not nearly as much, as indeed we are ignorant of the more general nomos-building attributes of the 'subject' knowledge which children imbibe).

This sort of information would have to be collected at great expense, over long periods of time and possibly in ways that might fundamentally 'pollute' (via the presence of the investigatory process) the learning processes themselves. Does the degree of difficulty help *partly* explain (no one would question the existential sincerity of the beliefs held) the 'populism' of some recent methodological prescription? (Bartholomew, 1974; Whitty and Young, 1975).

Virtually all the research which we have on schools, then, is predicated upon the notion that they do (because they should) perform universal good. When schools are found to be doing things like producing hostility among lower stream fourth formers or transmitting 'non-relevant' content to them, we tend to be irresistibly invited even *qua* sociologists to draw the conclusion that they are 'failing'. This is a profoundly unsociological stance and indexes the extent both to which education is value saturated and sociological perspectives contain inexplicated value premises; and, too, why one-scene works of research have disproportionate influence (the compulsion of morality is not that of mere evidence) and the searing aspect of *exposé* so often about them – devoted scientist accused of forcing Latin nouns on struggling twelve-year-old; I was a victim of group learning on the yellow table, says flaxen-haired Sandra.

What we have: the society of pupils

Lambert's and his associate's work on boarding education had perhaps most successfully avoided this indulgence. They did not set out to collect curricular or classroom organization data, but have in an unsentimental and unprejudiced way analysed boarding-school activities as pursuing instrumental, expressive and organizational goals (Lambert, 1966, 1975). They allowed children to talk for themselves about the meaning of school to them (Lambert *et al.*, 1968), and attempted to relate their views to adult perspectives. They make perhaps their most interesting contribution in terms of evidence upon the relationship between 'formal' and 'informal social systems' in schools. By the 'informal system', they mean 'the pattern of norms, values and relationships not prescribed ... by the

144

official goals of the organization, but which still have effects on these goals' (Lambert *et al.*, 1973: 298). Both pupils and staff create an 'informal society' of their own. The much more highly studied world of pupils is one where the norms can vitally affect how the individual relates to the school's official goals.

In boarding schools, which they argue frequently have many of the features of the total institution (Goffman, 1961), the informal pupil system may sometimes soften, sometimes intensify, the rigours of the official – 'in many schools where the pains of imprisonment are at a minimum, particularly in progressive schools, the informal pupil system is strongly developed ... schools ... with the highest degree of comfort and privacy also had very strong informal systems' (Lambert *et al.*, 1973: 299). Indeed, in general, their finding was that 'when the structural variables of schools are constant, their pupils societies seem to differ markedly' (p. 300). Rigid streaming did not necessarily alienate the lower groups, coercive control create alienation or high 'totality' produce uniform pupil adaptation. They summarize – 'where the official system is weak there will always be a strong society, but where the official system is strong, the pupil society may be weak, as in public schools, or strong, as in progressive schools, senior approved schools and service training establishments'. Changes in pupil society will occur as a result of outside, wider societal influences, but the relations between formal and informal systems tend to be cyclical or to oscillate over time, to go through 'good' and 'bad' patches. They suggest an unexplored area of 'functional alternative'-ness, whereby informal systems in some schools serve needs provided for elsewhere in others. They note the capacity of such systems to be sparked off, 'crystallized' by small, individual events and suggest that informal systems have cultural resilience and continuity, no doubt partly of a self-fulfilling kind.

Keep your feet off the desk in your head

What does this work tell us? It suggests in a school world populated by hybrid Parsonian-interactionist men (and pupils), that when grown-ups set out to do it distinctively one way,

145

the complex dynamics of the organization will tend to produce reactions, opposites and unexpected 'accommodations' among pupils. The public (or by extension, comprehensive or infant) school world is not only not what it seems but it is likely to be not what anyone quite set out to achieve. The play between intention and actuality is constant: it is open to outside influence as well as internal realignment even in relatively 'cut-off' institutions. In more open ones, it is liable to relatively rapid alteration, though what we know about time scales in educational change is very limited indeed. Schools, like any human institution, are not just what they seem to be. They tend traditionally to be particularly hierarchical, people changing (but remember that there is no unilateral influence without reciprocation), communal-living (hence peer-group influenced) settings. They have atmosphere or consciously sought 'ethos' and their mood or 'tone' fluctuates. Little things can become disproportionately inflated, yet we do not know a great deal sociologically about what does what in terms of the relations between intended or unintended organizational practice and pupil response and identity. In public schools such as those studied by Lambert, drawing from a restricted range by class or origin and sharing relatively homogenous background assumptions and aspirations, we know that pupils in the same organization vary right across the board in terms of types of attachment and response to what their experience is all about. When we get to studies that purport to tell us how school rives children along the lines of class, ability and ambition perhaps we might allow this to remind us that these do not exhaust personality and identity factors. The fine print of social organization carries meaning which the conceptual typeset may only distract us from.

To put it plainly, adults in schools plan grouping patterns and pastoral systems and the extra-curricular and rules and sanctions which, in some combination, square with their values and quiet expediency (never forgetting the demands of Topsy, the goddess of educational arrangements). The message systems created for pupils are usually complex and always have the character of judging worth. Whereas we need to know what particular combinations of groups, contents, pedagogy

146

and general ethos *do* to differing children by way of formation and control – if ever there was an agonizing and tendentious research programme, here it is – what we have is studies of pupil peer-relations and subcultures. We can situate the origin of these easily enough with a touch of technological determinism (the early invention of the sociometric test), political insight (it is easy to get at the children, harder at adults even social class for social class) and historical empathy (the equality story ran on naturally from children's background investigations to what streaming did to group perceptions and treatment). But while we know a good deal about the general control exercised by peer expectations we have yet to do the work which tells us whether doing mixed ability maths, where content has been arranged in a series of discrete non-overlapping topics (a collection within a subject in Bernstein terminology) to allow for the fact that not completing any previous one must not interfere technically with the right to and chance of beginning the next at the calendar date specified on equal conceptual terms, matters more. One suspects that it does.

Lambert's work, of course, never set out to collect curricular and classroom information in any detail. Yet I have begun with it, because it has two overriding virtues. First of all, it polarizes the agony of organizational (and sociological) work. In general terms it shows that when you think that you can see the hidden hand, you know that you're talking either sociology or nonsense. There is no *a priori* way of distinguishing the two. In research terms, if it sounds like news one should turn it over, test and retry it, for it could well be sociology. If you suspect that it has 'got' to be true, it's probably morality or nonsense. However, there is always the long shot that it might be the equivalent in sociological terms of 'the sun must rise'. In a world where we are all Popperians now, we know that it *does not have to* but nevertheless that we can put our stochastic shirts on it. Getting sociological news is difficult, and worth a bit of smudgy print, and Lambert and his colleagues' work provides some. It also carries the additional bonus of being school-comparative in an area where most of our organization work is in single case study form, even upon pupil sub-cultures.

The venerable grandparent of all school studies is Waller's interactionist classic of 1932. This is not an empirical study as such, but is highly informed by detailed knowledge of high schools. Waller's high schools have 'wishes' which cannot be neatly coincident with those of parents and pupils. Being 'universalistic', the school cannot provide an absolute version of 'best' for everyone, so there is a fundamental *structural* antagonism between schools and parents. The reproductive task of the school drives it towards being a 'museum of virtue', transmitting the values of a generation back, a 'despotism poised in perilous equilibrium', threatened always by the strength of community and pupil society. He also shows the poignant price in 'apartness' that the American community still extracted from its teacher-priests in the thirties.

The original classic post-war case study in this tradition was Gordon's examination of Wabash High School. The ease with which the grade system's demands could be met, and the existence of a principal who believed that good teachers did not have control problems, led to a two-way trading system between teachers and pupils. Pupils sold performance for grades and teachers manipulated them in turn, particularly in the light of pupils' informal prestige system, to effect control. The study foreshadows others in attesting to the growth of the differentiating and control importance of the American extracurricular against the 'normality' of successful academic accomplishment.

The much misunderstood high-water mark in this research area was the comparison conducted by Coleman (1961) of ten schools of varying size (from one of 150 in a community of 1000 to some about 2000 strong in city and suburb), and class background (rural to 'executive'). Part of the misunderstanding stems from Coleman's own treatment of his data and its discussion. In his world, the family is losing its children in a society which has '*spawned*, something more than it bargained for' (1961: 4). 'The adolescent is *dumped* into a society of his peers' and *only* 53 per cent of them tick 'parents' when asked 'which of those things would be hardest for you to take – your parents' disapproval, your teachers' disapproval, or *breaking* with your friend' (p. 5) (all the italics in these quotes are mine

– and the other averaged figures for boys and girls are 3 per cent teachers, 43 per cent friends, with 'don't know' being an unavailable category). On the basis of the percentage of the 'leading crowd', i.e. the sociometric front-runners, in schools response under 'parents' falling to 49 per cent, Coleman avers that 'those students who are highly regarded by others are themselves committed in the adolescent group ...' (p. 6).

Given devices like this, methodologically and interpretationally, the study leaves a lot to be desired. But it is still possible to mine valuable insight from it. For instance, at 'Executive Heights', the upper-class school where college going after graduation was virtually universal, 'commitment' to academic matters *vis-à-vis* athletics, etc. was relatively very low. The school, regarded as being in the national top ten and into whose area parents deliberately moved so as to make it available to their children, was one where Coleman argued 'good grades are important for acceptance at the "right" college' (p. 80), and were nevertheless of vital moment for individual students and their parents, but where academic achievement counted for little and was devalued by the peer culture. In this school, deeply penetrated by societal and cultural influences, more than anywhere, pupils were 'impatient with the passive dependency that the school imposes upon them in its educational activities. They have been liberated by parents and by the worldliness that today's mass media bring, and are no longer pleased by the congratulations that follow good report cards. Their parents have liberated them, and the liberation is more social than intellectual' (p. 292). They focus their liberation on areas where they are free to act – from dating to drama – and within this area there is intense, parent-fed competition in terms of cars, clothes and courting, for peer-prestige. To say that the academic is unimportant here is to miss the entire importance of cultural and structural location.

In other schools, Coleman showed differing relative importance of grades, athletics, etc. and differing class composition of the student leadership. In each case what is demonstrated is the importance and strength in Lambert's terms of the informal system, given a 'weak' formal system whose core

149

is the historically evolved grade system admitting 'mass' success. The adolescent culture of each school is deeply marked by wider sources, as well as local community factors. Coleman's answer to the 'malaise' in terms of introducing 'academic competition' seems not to grasp that the competition would need to be underlined by scarcity of what the prizes would buy and the US higher education, high school output-receivers would hardly like that.

And your place in tracks or stream

The highly 'technologized' self-avowedly futuristic version of American high school process was described by Cicourel and Kitsuse (1963) in their study of 'Lakeshore High' – not unlike Coleman's 'Executive Heights' in being large, predominantly middle class and ambitious, with the student body again mainly college-going. They studied how the school's assorting process aligned student achievement with vocational or higher educational destiny via course assignation. A highly developed counselling system was described as itself creating or shaping 'talent' on the basis of the notions of under- or over-achievement. Pupils whose work habits and/or ambitions stood out of line with their 'objectively' test-revealed ability, constituted 'problems', whose aetiology was frequently sought in family-disjuncture or other sorts of 'clinically' interpreted factors. Efforts were made to achieve consonance between ability/aspiration and achievement, largely through assignation to what were deemed to be appropriate courses (and hence tracks).

Precise course choices – effectively of vital importance for high-status college-going – were important right from the start of the high school career. Certain courses were barred to those not doing well enough on entry tests, so that there were, in effect, three different college preparatory programmes, entailing relatively homogeneous ability grouping or 'tracking'. Cicourel and Kitsuse's general comment upon the process, mindful of Turner's depiction of contest mobility in the US, is that while aspirants' efforts are relevant 'to qualifying them for the "contest" ... their efforts are not necessarily evaluated, as might be assumed, by academic standards alone'. In terms of

150

test-scores and grades 'students who show such effort may be handicapped or even excluded from the "contest"'.

Progress 'is contingent upon the interpretations, judgements and action of school personnel vis-à-vis the student's biography, social class and "social type" as well as his demonstrated ability and performance' (pp. 135–6). The judgements concerned maturity, emotional stability, character and personal appearance, accommodated in a bureaucratic setting that amounted, in the author's judgement, to sponsorship. Students were, in the end, though, assisted to enter college if their parents insisted upon it, even if the school's judgement was that this was unsuitable. But they contend the school in effect did have a great deal of control over the precise advice concerning individual students which got to the 125 college recruitment representatives who visited the school each year.

The great bulk of sociological research work on British state schools is also about their most obvious, equality related, organizational features, ability grouping and its effects. 'Streaming' has long been a highly pervasive phenomenon, starting quite early in the junior school and being almost universal by the age of 11. Our secondary system has, of course, been traditionally 'streamed' both by and within institutions. As Bernstein suggests, and Nash attests (see below), children imbibe a deeply held ability identity very early on in their primary school career, and have their secondary school career determined very much in terms of it. Hargreaves (1967) has shown in a secondary modern context how successive streaming and restreaming of non-remedial children in a school over four years (school exam success and behaviour being used as criteria) produced four fourth year (A–D) streams, strongly differentiated pro- and anti-school, given to very different work habits, friendship patterns and so on. His children are interactionist with a rather Parsonian *penchant* for imbibing or inverting legitimate value systems. We can understand them better taking Wheeler's (1966) point that serial collective intakes (a very large number of similar cases once a year) provide the perfect seed-bed for group-solidarity problem solving which is perfected like a rod kept in pickle, by such schools themselves. Their devotion to twin-ness of

151

'ability/effort' with 'good/bad behaviour' produces practices which positively band together the 'less-able' *plus* anti-school 'bright', into unmanageable 'sink-streams', where the social dynamics of Gouldner's (1954) punishment centred rule-system (if they don't obey them, make some more, enforce them harder) produces explosive resentment and rejection.

In Hargreaves's study, as in some degree in Lambert's, and Cicourel and Kitsuse's, the traditional fall-back of class will not serve to explain child differences, given the homogeneity of their schools' intakes. At least, if family differences *do* explain some of them, they exist at a level of delicacy or in a range not tapped by the data. Not all of the low-streamers in Hargreave's study are anti-school, or the high ones pro- it. But in Werthman's terms (1971) we can say that most of the D-streamers do not accept many of schools' demands as legitimate or to be taken seriously, except as consequences directly follow. To adapt Geer's useful idea (1968), it may be that their conceptions of the area in which teacher may pronounce legitimately has shrunk. School has at least lost the power to engage their attention for much of its official purposes, and the social learning (and control) involved concerning authority and participation is no doubt distinctive, though we cannot by any means be sure about its outcome in wider, non-school senses.

Lacey's study of a grammar school (King's, 1969, work is also of relevance), presents a quite different picture. The initial pressure of academic and behaviour demands made by school press quite acutely upon some children – all of whom were junior-school 'best pupils' – to create quite poignant problems of individual adaptation. But group solutions do not notably emerge. The original random assignation of boys to teaching groups in the first year gives way to streaming (including an 'express', four-years-to-'O' level group) in the second year. By this time, children have been 'differentiated' by their various subject teachers, and globally by the school, in terms of work and 'behaviour' criteria. There is a degree of anti-school attitude polarization in middle school (Lacey had to change his research group as his original plan to 'follow through' was unhinged by change in school grouping policy, so the evidence is not really sequential), but what he describes as unifying coffee-bar culture and, perhaps more importantly, the clear instrumental benefits flowing from attachment to work requirements, kept the vast majority of pupils in this sense, 'pro-school'.

Himmelweit and Swift's (1969) work on 11+ 'marginals' attests very strongly to the school-allocated-to phenomenon being much more important than precise IQ, class or other family variables influencing secondary performance and careers of a large cohort which they followed through. This study of children, who, in effect, because of imprecision of allocation procedures 'might' have gone to grammar school or not, is most interesting as a comment on the importance of the connection between the strength and the standing of differing school social systems.

The work of Brandis and Young (1967) has also been unduly neglected, showing as it does that relatively strong streaming practices can have highly favourable outcomes, on balance, in certain social class school intake circumstances. In view of the present intimations that 'staying on' and going to higher education are not on necessarily perpetual increase, the importance of their arguments is increased. Their general conceptual point that schools will group differently if they define their main problem as one of 'retention' or 'performance' in respect of pupils is of continuing interest and has not yet received the research attention which it deserves.

Banks and Finlayson, taking tradition sociological and psychological approaches to a logical, but unusual, interdisciplinary conclusion in respect of the educational achievement careers of parallel groups in grammar and comprehensive schools, demonstrate 'that the school can, under certain circumstances be *more important* than home background in explaining differences in school achievement' (1973: 187). Thus they again, importantly, attack the Plowden heresy and, equally interesting, show that their comprehensive groups did better than the grammar school group, controlled for ability, even though the grammar school boys had superior socio-economic status. Thus they complexify the hallowed social class and family simplicities, only to raise fresh problems about the school – in this case no doubt residing in the differing fate of

153

'best' comprehensive and 'ordinary' grammar school pupils being compared. But even so, they reveal something not evident in the Himmelweit and Swift study. This highly distinctive British literature is all of a piece with the emerging problems of our system discussed historically above and conceptualized by Turner and his successive elaborators. The controlling and formative power of education is located largely in global selection for and within institutions. It belongs between the output of the home and the input of the occupational system above. We may argue about the precise importance of ages and stages and institutions, but the message is that the system controls early and slabbily by managing identity via assignation to levels in an ability hierarchy (double combed for 'behaviour'). We must watch out for its simplistics, for no one has yet done the case study of the secondary modern that made it, streamed or unstreamed.

All about equality

Even at the level of case studies there is a sense in which the British educational eye can only marvel at the degree of sensitivity displayed and attention paid in Lakeshore High to the identification and channelling of 'talent'. The crudity of British academic and social typing is quite profound in comparison. There are lessons of other sorts to be learned too, particularly in respect of a growth in 'mixed ability' organizational types, especially when there is something approaching an all-ability entry. Teachers and pupils *have* to 'make sense' of one anothers' behaviours – they assign one anothers' activities to types, they label persons. Social interaction itself presupposes such meaning assignation and once initiated, is conducted in relation to it. All educational situations are such that public, organized information is available upon which typing by teachers may be based – traditionally ability and achievement measures – as well as personal view. In this sort of setting, where 'ability' is plenitudinous, as in Lakeshore High, we should expect much the same social effect as in a situation where ability was in chronically short supply (or where differences in it have been put to the ideological sword by staff members): that is, that children will be differentiated upon *other* than ability criteria. Perhaps effort or application will be chosen, for they have high classroom relevance. Possibly, if these too are set aside as suffering taint of social class bias, only the 'clinical' may remain as respectable science-professional ground. In how many open-plan, open-group, open-curriculum schools is the explanation for children's motivation given detailed interpretation in terms of personality-family syndromes of health and pathology? (Mix in class as well for the perfect 'overdetermined pupil'.) Clearly there are further alternatives too: creativity, bluntness, egocentricity, resentment of authority and so on, can become in degree (and combination), publicly defined and valued attributes in school and classroom, some more easily than others, given the management and resource problems inherent in the conventional limits of our schools. But we must realize that there is always a strain towards defensibility and fairness of action in publicly accountable institutions. Moreover, the qualities required by success criteria are in large measure capable of being worked upon, once known. Unto him that hath shall different be added by parents sharp as to what it takes.

Upon the same general principle of scepticism, we need to look carefully at the penetrating simplicities of Ford and her co-workers' discussion of 'working class culture', and its effect upon autonomy and role-playing. Their argument is that historic conditions of scarcity have produced circumstances in which 'distribution within the household is governed by rationing' (Ford *et al.*, 1967: 68), whose 'imperatives favour distribution according to ascribed statuses of age, sex and familial function', leading to a 'right and proper' model of justice and 'friendship as a dense area of reciprocal rights and duties based on parity', being internalized. These patterns assume 'cultural autonomy' even in the absence of original scarcity, producing children 'who do not gain universally valid interpersonal behaviour techniques such as role distance' (p. 70), that is, who can *play* but not *play at* roles. While not denying the perceptiveness of the basic insight, there must be every reason to doubt, except in the context of continuing 'scarcity' (poverty exists), the argument as to cultural autonomy and neatness of class basis. The experience of a variety of segmented audiences by children is universal in our culture – of home, school, friends, etc. – and to this extent, the retreat from one to another is possible. The vision of '*the* working class child' in need of school-assisted dramaturgical skills is as over-generalized and mechanical as all statements about that category, and less lovely. Goffman's man is more than usually an attribute, not a whole person.

The hard fact remains, though, that to organize school as if the incoming clientele were equal in all relevant respects would be as unfair to assume the inherent inequality of its possible parts. It is a battle between the former view over the normalcy of the latter which has marked much recent writing on schools. It was institutionalized in the early part of the original version of an enormously important Open University course on *School and Society*. Its appeal can be derived most easily from Dale's (1973) advocacy of a 'phenomenological approach to the school, which starts from paying attention to things only as they appear to us ... leads ... to a stress on the actor's subjective understanding of the social world ...' and '... analysis at a micro, or social psychological level', with the actor's interpretation as paramount (p. 196). We must hold our preconceptions in suspense, even in the study of schools talk of 'learning' or 'playing' in terms valid to members (children, not teachers), showing how they generate and maintain their activities. Thus the sociologist can accomplish 'de-reification' of his own traditional categories. When we talk in Hopper's terms of 'warming up' and 'cooling out', Dale suggests that 'it is at least conceivable that the individuals involved may see the situation rather differently' (p. 179).

If this approach is coupled with an interactionism which does not assume that actors arrive on study scenes supposition-less, plus a recognition of 'characteristic features which severely delimit the possible definitions of school situations' (p. 180) for example, like legal restraints, then a negotiative power model is possible. This is particularly useful for schools, where pupils involuntarily present 'may thus be led to a greater awareness of the constructed, imposed nature of the school world' and for teachers for whom 'the social world of the school may be no less consciously constructed' (p. 181) –

the key question becoming 'which members carry over what meanings from what other social groups?'

Dale goes on to argue that such an approach is oriented towards penetrating the 'deep structure' of the classroom world, and a link-up with the 'sociology of knowledge'. While both of these things may be in some measure true, it is likely that the most important thing about the approach is that 'it makes explicit that much of what happens, much of what is assumed about social situations by those interacting in them, is accountable for only in terms of actors' biographies and their own identities' (p. 184). The deep structure of *this* message is that history, class, hierarchy are dead. By adopting the correct 'paradigm' – the phenomenological one – teachers may institutionalize (if that is not a contradiction in terms) this end. It is a powerful message of personal salvation. It has run through recent debate on 'cultural deprivation' and has sought to turn practical constraint into morality. But if part of the *meaning* of school is the imposition of generality and normality in a culture, its purpose is both to make children more alike and more different. The question continues to be, therefore, where is the school contingently unfair or unduly pejorative of children who come bearing *differing* attributes to attempt success in its terms? The only additional question possible that will not confound the enterprise is what must school do to make success more widely available or access to it more possible? Any economist worth his salt would neither rule out vertical integration backward towards the source of supply or forward towards the market. But if the product be bad ...

The classroom awaits

Teachers expect, children are labelled

Expectations is what we have plenty of. The recent (already classic, meaning among other things that its virtues are for many of its consumers beyond disconfirmation) scene-setter in this area has been Rosenthal and Jacobson's (1968) work. They found it possible to increase the short-run test scores of some elementary school children of mainly white and Chicano

157

background in a predominantly lower class, urban Californian school by deluding their teachers that they had administered to the pupils a test which predicted 'blooming' or 'spurting', i.e. sudden immanent improvement in their work. The children were in fact administered an ordinary (here is part of the rub – a possibly inappropriate, see Snow, 1969) test, some of them being randomly designated improvers. Teachers were given their names, but asked not to 'do anything different' with them. An unspecified amount of checking went on to ensure that this latter instruction was carried out and lo! (the whole thing is presented very much as a bit of not-understood interpersonal magic), the scores improved for virtually everyone in the school, but disproportionately for certain sorts of 'experimentals', falling back on subsequent retests. The study is thoroughly unsatisfactory so far as telling us anything as to 'why it happened', and has largely failed at replication. It has touched a nerve, however, hardly as completely satisfied since the democratic thrill of Lewin, Lippitt and White's mask-making experiment. Both feed the same powerful impulse.

Common sense yells at us that expectations held become action (even if of a subtle interpersonal kind) and reaction to produce cumulative effects. A whole generation of social psychological experimentation from Asch to Milgram tell us that even in the least propitious and most resistant looking laboratory milieu, judgement and feeling can be altered even by profoundly false information, if certain behavioural props are knocked out or put in. But nothing don't make nothing.

Pygmalion notwithstanding then, what of the classroom evidence? Against the background of an investigation of teaching infants to read and reading-readiness, Goodacre found differences 'between the teacher evaluations of the children's reading ability and the children's tested performance' (1971: 12). In particular, upper working-class children did better on tests than would be expected from evaluations (based on book-level reached). This puzzle led to an investigation of teacher attitudes, which revealed that teachers did attach importance to background, particularly in respect of the provision of suitable material at home. 'Good' homes tended to be seen in more motivational and cultural terms (imparting interest to the child orienting him towards the teacher's role), 'poor' in more material terms. They were regarded as particularly important in distinguishing the 'two' working-class levels. They differed somewhat by teacher's age and degree of authoritarianness.

Teachers picked up plenty of clues about economic and material home background, though they were not as reliable in estimating lower occupational categories and newer professions. In lower working-class areas, they tended to see their school classes as homogeneous groups socially *and* intellectually and to believe that they had no children of above average ability in the class. Goodacre comments '... their own language system and academically biased education might make it extremely difficult for many of them to recognize unfamiliar forms of mental functioning' (p. 12). Teachers had much more difficulty in making evaluations of all sorts in upper working-class schools, as in combined infant–junior departments (as opposed to infant only schools). In lower working-class schools, they appeared to lower overall their scale of normal expectations. Infant teachers as a group saw themselves as unambitious, happy and cheerful. They were predominantly from intermediate and skilled manual backgrounds and were first generation professionals, Goodacre suggests perhaps not very fluent 'as spokesmen for their pupils' educational needs' (p. 13). The type of school, occupational position and personality characteristics of teachers were much more important than class of origin.

The general impression is, then, of teachers having high/low class stereotypes, with more fluidity in the middle. They placed a lot of weight on environmental factors generally but with insufficiently explored 'organizational' differences patterning their proclivities (see also Barker-Lunn, 1973; and Morrison and McIntyre, 1973). It is hard to sustain any simplistic view of infant teacher as psychometrician at this general level of the survey.

What are we trying to hide?

Nash (1973), driven on by a secondary school experience where all was not what it appeared to be, guided by *Pygmalion*

159

and the NFER, found a mixed social class, unstreamed, infant–junior school in order to focus upon pupil–teacher interaction as the real source of children's knowledge of the relative status of each (including their own) pupil in the class. Even in the classroom which he studied where 'the group teaching method could scarcely be bettered ... pupils were still able to tell exactly which group was higher than another and which children were better or worse off than they' (pp. 14–15). Nash observes that 'There is a sense, therefore, in which it can be said that schools teach hierarchical levels of personal worth more successfully than anything else' (p. 16). He suggests that the message system is the classroom technology – groups, book levels, difficulty of number work, which are ordered and 'read' with great accuracy by children and 'fit' extremely well with teacher's rank orders. He puts forward the need for personal consistency as the possible engine of the interactive process, once started.

Nash chooses Repertory Grid Analysis as a major technique to try to maximize the own-choiceness of teachers' views of children, while still permitting their quantified comparison. He claims that its use enabled a demonstration of the school's deserved child-centred reputation and a questioning of 'working class handicap' explanations for there was no easy fit between bestowal of teacher-view making for success or failure and class background. In a second phase of his research, where he followed children through from last year of junior into first year of comprehensive school, he locates the phenomenon of primary and secondary schools 'overshooting' one another in attempts to effect continuity. Boys transferring from 'strict' top junior to 'progressive' first year secondary classrooms were significantly affected in terms of lowered effort and classroom behaviour.

Altogether, Nash is very much impressed by the power of teacher images, transferred into practice and applied over weeks and years to a child, in terms of creating that child's self-image. One can only agree that the business of 'how social background factors become translated into differential actions in the classroom' (p. 90), must involve the study of self-concept development over long periods of time such as

Brookover (1962) showed. Teacher expectations do not simply jump interactive gaps, like hot sparks, to effect child behaviour. Rather, they are part of a network of ongoing pressures, other sources of which are from the individual child's point of view, self and peers as well as parents and other adults, which sustain and alter feelings and identity. Without doubt, individual teachers can have powerful influence for individual good or evil. But we need to recognize that as children do become older, 'significant others' tend to increase in total and thin out. Individual teachers can be coped with as 'crazy' or 'great' and their subject live or die. Children may become very skilled at coping with teacher variation, but that by the time they can do so well, self-concepts are likely to be driven very deep. And as we observed in relation to Ford et al.'s view, this is not likely to be neatly class differentiated. There are crucial points, however, at which we may well tend to ask too much, particularly of 'middling' ability children. For example, at secondary transfer the thrust into a whole gamut of pedagogical regimes or classroom ethoses can cause difficulty, as the 'inexperienced' teachers, punitively dealt-towards that Nash observed, will no doubt agree. Such variation may have a great deal more to do with difficulty which children encounter at transfer than the change from weak to stronger framing which Nash thinks will have typically taken place in the junior school well before transfer, or increasing number of teachers, subjects or rooms themselves.

Nash's study is set firmly in the interactionist–anthropological tradition. He is committed in the same way as Jackson (1968) is to a view of elementary classrooms as complex and potentially highly abrasive interaction scenes of some intensity, duration and pervasiveness for children. Here and now, teacher is caught in the double bind of socializer and evaluator. Pupils are often bored, crowded and increasingly adept at managing the impression of attending. Regardless of content, the children are imbibing a 'hidden curriculum' of some importance to their ability to live with the demands of industrial society.

These are the same sort of classrooms that Henry (1955a) described as ideally devoted to 'spiralling', 'polyphasic' learning (that is, open-ended, and of more than one thing at a time) in the American elementary school. In them, the independent observer can all too often see not only that there is a hidden curriculum of accompanying activity, but that the overt intentions of teacher become displaced by them. Children learn to pick up and distinguish intended messages and the accompanying 'noise'. Indeed, a great deal of Henry's work shows the complex connections between teacher and children's behaviour as expressions of what *both* need and are culturally programmed to provide. 'Trading for affect' in classrooms whose real 'no choice' function 'is to prevent the truly creative from getting out of hand' (1966: 286), where there 'must therefore be more of the caveman than of the spaceman about our teachers' (p. 288), is a constant process, along with the 'conventional' one of knowledge transmission. The 'real nature' of the curriculum becomes the open question, but always against the anthropological reality of education in all cultures acting to shape and narrow the perceptual field 'through emphasizing only certain things'. However, given the polyphasic nature of learning, 'the process will never be completely effective and the resultant educational failure must be one of the sources of socio-cultural conflict and change' (p. 175). Education, then, is an incomplete replicator, except in 'very stable cultures' or within the ideological world of Marxist exegesis (whose end such cultures may be).

Too permeable for words?

Jackson, in his study of American elementary teachers especially chosen for their professionally-adjudged excellence, found that classroom expertise coexisted with an inability to rationalize the very categories of child-centred discourse. His sample taught through the seats of their skirts. Sharp and Green (1975) in a study of more than usual theoretical reflection, have focussed in great detail upon three infant classrooms in 'Mapledene School' where staff were viewed by their headmaster as being 'very stable' and 'above average enthusiasm, commitment and competence'. Their substantive intention was to 'focus upon the "child-centred" approach to education and ... to study and demonstrate some of the more or less subtle ways in which wider social structural "forces" impinge upon or influence the pedagogy and other social processes at the classroom and school levels' (1975: vii). They show that the child-centred pedagogue produces effects in terms of the hierarchical differentiation of pupils much like any other teacher and that there are strong structural blockages in the way of actualizing a 'developmental' approach. Teachers in their studies were 'subject to conflicting expectations and ambivalences stemming from several sources' (p. 216) in a child-centred context whose chief organizational property was wide child discretion so long as activity 'satisfied the conditions for "busyness"'. Developmental vocabulary ('needs', 'readiness', etc.) went in want of apt indicators beyond common sense, teachers falling back upon the rationales of 'happiness' or 'what children do they need to do', with strong therapeutic/deprivation undertones. They summarize: 'The teachers are able to organize the environment of their classrooms to allow a wide range of choice but have to generate their own theory of instruction for the children.' Teaching traditional skills, to which the school was also committed was very difficult, for teachers were faced with highly differentiated child abilities and the necessity to 'develop it from within'.

In practice, 'pupil teacher intersubjectivity is low' (p. 218), a matter of some moment for the viability of a 'knowing the child' regime. 'Certain pupils are being denied 'their reality' and the opportunity to orient themselves towards the hidden curriculum' (p. 218). Certain pupil identities were hardened and in respect of control 'disequilibrium in the structure of classroom relations was more likely to occur with the "bright", "ideal client" than with the "dim" or "really peculiar" child who presented fewer problems. The former were more capable of exposing the reality of power and control underlying the child-centred harmony of the classroom' (p. 219). The control of pupils and the formation of their careers are admixed from this early stage, and from the start emerge with variable negotiability out of teachers' types, pupils' power and the frequency of their interaction.

It is central to Sharp and Green's purpose to show how Mapledene's classrooms are involved in the process of reproducing economic, social and cultural systems, are indeed shot through with wider structural pressures. They believe 'the view of society as continually in process, open to reconstruction and continual modification' to be 'an ideological illusion'. Situations may be such where 'the individual may find it very difficult to give a meaning to his situations or actions at all' – he may be completely constrained (p. 27). Their Marxian-influenced perspective prompts them to want to analyse specific contexts, like schools and classrooms, as part of a wider totality. They see the origin of social and knowledge stratification in the classrooms which they observe as well as the maintenance of social control via induction into 'appropriate attitudes and modes of action'.

They do not see their findings as specially indexing anything historically unusual in Mapledene. In terms of intended outcome–actual practice, disjunction ever was education's fate. But they do suggest 'that the educational ideology of child-centred progressivism fails to comprehend the realities of a given situation of a stratified society where facilities, prestige and rewards are unequally distributed' (p. 226), that it involves an 'emotional turning away' from society to the regenerative power of individual consciousness, which they believe entombs its protagonists as the 'unwilling victims of a structure that undermines the moral concerns that they express'. The way out is hard, and as yet undeveloped.

Mapledene is, without doubt, a somewhat forbidding place. One needs almost to remind oneself that people – adults and children – survive it, daily. In this sense, Sharp and Green's conjunction of Durkheim – for much of their conceptualization draws deeply upon the same sources as Bernstein's vision of invisible pedagogy – and Marx, has something of the same effect as on Bourdieu. While the study does therefore, bring together very powerfully a number of disparate macro-theoretical considerations and plays them upon the analysis of a single institution, as well as along the way mercifully quietening the existential chatter, the overdetermined silence is a little bit deafening. Parents of Mapledene unite – schools were never as 'efficient' as this. Let us resample your wares in 1984 so as to try to judge the gap between grown-up shock and the ignorance of childhood which protects us all.

Where Mapledene is seen to work in societal context, Rist's well known and longer-available study attended to the same processes of how young children are stratified (in classrooms), but with no gloss on teacher's 'initial presuppositions'. Rist follows dwindling portions of a kindergarten class through for two and a half years and three teachers in a blighted, urban area school in America. The school has a 98 per cent black population, with more than half the families of children in the school on public welfare support. The story is by now familiar. First black teacher allocates seats in what appears to be in accordance with her 'mixed black–white, well-educated middle class' (Rist, 1970: 422) normative reference group and her own godly, civil-rights oriented background. She is reported as saying that the majority of children 'just had no idea of what was going on in the classroom' (p. 424), and examples are given of her actions as according perfectly well with a notion of inducting the bereft into cultural propriety, while believing 'that some can do it and some cannot' (p. 425). Seats were assigned after eight day attendance on three tables, observably distinguished by clothing, degree of being called upon for help, physical proximity, degree of verbal interaction with the teacher, differences in odour, degree of darkness of skin, hair condition, leadership behaviour and use of standard English as opposed to black dialect. Once created, the situation worsens, the initial assignment becoming the 'reason' for teachers two and three for future placement. Children may have come bearing mixed potential but teacher quickly carries out 'society's task' of ensuring caste-like differentiation. Rist believes that the teachers may have operated on the assumption that only a portion of the class could be saved from ghetto-fate, and that part of this mechanism resides in their learning to define some of their peers as having pariah status. Why didn't he ask?

While there is no doubt great tragedy involved in Rist's classrooms for those doomed to teachers' disfavour and 'secondary learning', one wonders exactly what 'complicity' the school 'strongly shares in maintaining poverty and unequal opportunity', in the light of Sharp and Green's logic. The air of 'forgive them not for they know what they do' symptomatizes an unlovely amount of research whose ethic is ostensibly phenomenological *agape*. It is hardly sociology.

Sorry, you'll just have to wait

Rist's view that 'there is a greater tragedy than being labelled as a slow learner and that is being treated as one' (p. 448), might well be echoed in aspect of Keddie's case study of fourth year humanities teaching in a large, mixed, streamed, class-heterogeneous comprehensive. In this school, an explicit attempt was being made to offer 'an undifferentiated programme across the ability range' (1971: 133) via an inquiry-based plus key lesson and workcard method, in this curriculum area. The school was depicted as generally atypical in terms of its high degree of innovation, and the humanities department taught its children in bands and looked 'forward to teaching completely mixed ability groups' (p. 134). However, C stream pupils presented 'teachers with problems of social control and in the preparation and presentation of teaching material'. The humanities department was, Keddie suggests, committed to a largely environmentalist view of intelligence, motivation as the main source of ability, and was against streaming and a differentiated curriculum.

Their new course was devised in the hope of helping pupils to become 'more autonomous and rational beings' (p. 137). But Keddie believed that, in fact, from the start it catered for 'the A stream academic and middle-class pupil' (though she does not seem to know what the class proportions in the streams are), implicitly pointing towards 'working at your own speed' in a structured course encouraging competitive, autonomous response and oriented vocationally towards higher education. Her picture, then, of teachers unable to carry their high 'educationalist' ideals into actuality.

What appeared to stand in the way, was the 'dominant organizing category of what counts as ability', which lay behind the school's banding–streaming system, and which they shared with their non-humanities colleagues – indeed, which made their interaction with them possible. In its terms, normal attributes were assigned to A, B and C pupils, and in respect of the latter, generated conflict. This was solved by teacher 'attempting to render pupil definitions invalid' (p. 139), tidying up gaps left by ability-motivation explanations with social class categorization. This led to a situation where 'what teachers "know" about pupils as social, moral and psychological persons is extended to what they know about them as intellectual persons...' (p. 143). Thus is the curriculum differentiated: 'Material is categorized in terms of its suitability for a given ability band and, by implication, ability is categorized in terms of whether or not these pupils can manage the material' (p. 144). Acquiring concepts along with being able to grasp the 'mode of inquiry' became the lines along which differentiation is justified.

Keddie implies that teachers do not allow for, or regard as relevant, 'that A and C pupils tend to approach knowledge from different positions and with different expectations' (p. 146), but rather that they confuse this with lack of intelligence or motivation or the existence of hostility in C pupils, and their converses for As. It is assumed that C pupils cannot master subjects, require more examples and cannot 'make it' with difficult concepts. A band pupils 'take over' teacher's definitions, work within subject frameworks, learn 'what questions may be asked within a particular subject perspective' (p. 151), unlike C streamers. The latter may be blockaged, Keddie suggests, by difficulty in suspending the relevance or appropriateness of everyday meanings and in the ability to argue by negative case. However, in many of the examples she gives, it is quite possible that the 'first-timeness' of the curricular and pedagogical exercise and particularly the unfamiliarity with some material shown by subject teachers attempting to span unfamiliar areas, exacerbated these sorts of difficulty. Keddie underplays this in favour of emphasizing the possible salience of failure stemming from the difficulty that some children have in 'putting away' their everyday knowledge. Such pupils are, presumably, most damaged by the 'use to which the school puts knowledge' so as 'to establish that subjects represent the way about which the world is normally known in an "expert" as opposed to a "common sense" mode'.

Rist and Keddie share the view that what goes on in class-rooms has much to do with the transmission of social class position. Rist communicates a deeply felt dislike for the operations of his middle-class teachers in accomplishing their classroom management at the cost of some children's self-respect and progress (we infer). We do not know how 'usual' his teachers are, but we suspect in the light of Sharp and Green's analysis that they are not alone as their malaise is structural rather than (or in addition to being) personal, nor do we know how in the long run their pupils are marked by their treatment, and we cannot compare the effects with 'untracked' classrooms. Nash's work should lead us to suspect that Rist is talking in part about social psychological phenomenon which are modifiable rather than capable of abolition. His people are the pessimistic Frankensteins of several sorts of discourse, precipitated under the pressure of racism on understanding.

While Rist's analysis is emotionally bathed, Keddie's has all the impact of a rationally theorized bombshell. It is in fact marked by deep confusion and contradiction. It is confused over what is being distinguished 'sociologically' as between 'doctrine' (what teachers said that they would like to do ideally) and 'commitment' (what they actually did) as well as overloaded with pejorative connotation. It is contradictory in terms of her strong tacit urge shared with the young to bring down 'subjects' and erect 'common sense' as superior (or universal, it is the same thing) category, on account of the contingent trouble which some children get in transcending it. This represents the dark side of the recent 'sociology of knowledge' application to analysis, confusing the very real need to establish how knowledge comes to be differentially distributed (a form of life itself only given to the learned), with a presumption as to its 'badness' if its possession correlates unduly with superior social status. The people at this analysis are Marxmen searching for an ill-defined future in sociability beyond the proletarian revolution of the C band.

But of course, a further part of the trouble is the tendency, which we have shared in, to treat studies such as these as having produced 'findings' when, as Robinson (1974) points out, they stand a long way from a future when their plenitude

168

and comparability may make it possible 'to generate theoretical statements which have a wider application than to the study in which they were born' (p. 263). It is foolish to confuse the transient feeling that their heart is in the right place with the idea that they have transcended problems of evidence and bias.

I'll really give you something to think about in a minute

Nowhere are these problems more hotly contested than in the areas of language and deprivation. Let us be cautioned that 'our understanding of how language acts as a means of classroom learning is so limited that naturalistic studies of classroom language at present provide insights quite out of proportion to their size' (Barnes, 1971: 35) – shake hands with an old friend. Barnes is himself responsible for some of the best known work into 'the language of secondary education'. His work vividly illustrates the predominance of language, even in maths and science lessons, often not only to the detriment of pupils 'taking a more active part in manipulating materials, in planning and carrying out demonstrations, and in measuring and recording what they perceive' but in a way which *'has gone hand in hand with a failure to demand that they verbalize their learning*, that is, they use language as an active instrument for reorganizing their perception ... It is not that there is too much language, but that it is not fulfilling its functions as an instrument of learning. Rather *language is seen as an instrument of teaching'* (Barnes *et al.*, 1971: 66).

Differential attentiveness of pupils to the control aspect of teacher's language *may* have important bearing upon their success, alongside their grasp of specialist languages which teacher presents and their ability to cope with the 'register of secondary education'. Barnes does not define the latter at all clearly, but it has to do obviously with the public segmenting of reality and conceptual processes within which pupils have to move from generality to precision. While nearly all the language which secondary teachers use in the classroom is elaborated code, the language of secondary education is not coterminus with it. Barnes suggests that practically perhaps, teachers can regard it 'as including those non-specialist forms of language which are outside the normal experience of eleven-year-old pupils' (p. 54). Though this experience varies widely, 'a lesson couched largely in such language will be beyond many pupils' comprehension'. Both its use and specialist terms, badly deployed, may stand in the way of learning.

Style, content and language are all of vital importance in classroom learning. Walker and Adelman (1975) show the complexity only too well in their discussion of 'whole class teaching'. Here teacher is highly visible, attempts to monitor all utterances, and everything said is potentially public. Teacher attempts to maintain the social context and use it to develop some idea, understanding or content (in other words the slowly dying archetype of classroom presentation). They suggest two important 'underlying qualities of control' in such situations: *definition* – *high* when 'the pupil is given a clear key with which to construct a response', *low* 'when the child has to create for himself a set of alternatives and then select an appropriate response which may be known only to himself': and *logical sequencing* of content – *closed* 'when there are tight logical steps between one item and the next', *open* 'when the pupil is involved in the negotiation of knowledge' (p. 47). These generate four kinds of talk strategies which they playfully label Cooks Tour (high, open) Freewheeling (low, open), and focussing (high, closed), leaving the fourth one mysteriously unnamed. Isn't that the promised land where necessity rules and freedom reigns where men come to the tight logical steps their own way?

Would you like your own room?

Grasping the hope that there could be a world where everything brought, every self-chosen step, led to more than solipsistic truth, in no way shortens the literature on 'cultural deprivation' which is as large now as it has long been polemical. It has been linked up with cross-cultural difference and seen as deeply implicated with language. Its conceptual origin has no doubt much to do with an over-easy (in hindsight) application of psychological categories to social and cultural areas – truly no one *can* be 'deprived' of their own culture.

Its appeal, translated into policy terms as 'compensatory

education' has, for differing reasons spanned diametrically opposed camps and has offered the prospects of 'control' and 'progress' (Friedman, 1967). It has long been accepted that for all sorts of reason – moral and sociological among them – talk of cultural 'difference' is apter than that of 'deficit'. It is recognized by all that children come to school bearing differences which make them differentially available to its demands. But there definitions and diagnosis part violently as to whether on the one hand school needs contingently to 'begin where children are' or on the other whether 'class' or 'ethnic' differences require institutionalization in something like educational apartheid, or alternatively surmounting by post-revolutionary 'reality'.

Bernstein's choice is for the first alternative. 'It is an accepted educational principle that we should work with what the child can offer. Why, then, don't we practice it? The introduction of the child to the universalistic meanings of public forms of thought is not compensatory education – *it is education*. It is in itself not making children middle class ...' However, at the same time, 'the implicit values underlying the form and content of the educational environment might' (Bernstein, 1971: 199). His view in effect rests upon the assumptions that 'we do not know what the child is capable of'. The class system is tied to but is not determinative of the production of elaborated and restricted speech variants (and their underlying codes). Code restriction applies to the *contexts* and *conditions* 'which will orient the child to universalistic orders of meaning' (p. 197), not to elaborated code production *altogether* (and vice versa). Elaborated code forms give explicit access to the principles and operations controlling object and person relationships through language. Bernstein's accompanying moral principle is uncomfortably Socratic, though his belief in the manifest power of the school to generate discontent is pessimistic.

Will the real working class please stand up?

The observations about language context and the class system (as revealed particularly in family control orientations) are based in Bernstein's case on a great deal of highly empirical work which has had an extremely wide take up. Rosen (1974) cites Bantock (1965), Jackson (1968) and Jensen (1969) as all claiming Bernstein-support for their very differing views, and the list could be much lengthened. Is the work powerfully general, vague or misunderstood?

In Rosen's case, when the clouds of rhetoric part, one level of disagreement can be seen to be over the true possession of insight into the nature and quality of 'working-class life'. Rosen rightly charges Bernstein with overgeneral use of class terms, which he would like corrected not by continual precise reference to the samples used in the reported research, but with a substitute Marxist vocabulary of 'the class system'. This would reveal 'that the linguistic capital of the dominant culture is persistently overvalued and that of the dominated culture undervalued' (1974: 67). Nothing divides the protagonists but their forms of thought. Bernstein insists that there is no moral or aesthetic difference between the codes but that possession or not of them contingently powerfully affects success in our school system, while Rosen returns to the naturalistic collection of 'working class' aesthetic output, daily confirming that it has complexity and beauty. He accepts Labov's revelation that the hemming and hawing, backing and filling, fashion-besotted speech of 'the middle class' continues to be the price paid 'for the acquisition of certain kinds of transactional language, and the loss of vitality and expressiveness, and obsession with proprieties' (p. 88). How overblown it all is! How easy it is to use the exigencies of class and racial relations to justify the virtues of noble linguistic savagery. How paradoxical, too, that the experience of such a belief should be given only to those who have lost the innocence which they extol.

Though parts of the force behind Rosen's objections stem from Marxist and literary sources, much else has flown from Labov's (1972) misunderstandings. For him 'Bernstein's views are filtered through a strong bias against all forms of working-class behaviour, so that middle-class language is seen as superior in every respect', as 'more abstract, and necessarily somewhat more flexible, detailed and subtle' (1972: 183). Is 'the average middle-class speaker ... the victim of sociolinguistic factors beyond his control'? Will Larry provide the quick, ingenious and decisive answer to hell on earth? Will the rising diphthong of Martha's Vineyard be deflected once more by further changes in the social structure? Is it true that nothing divides the researchers but their methodologies?

Labov, granting that 'a very great number of linguistic rules are not variable in the least' (p. 299; a view from which no linguist would demur), and emphasizing the basic necessity of considering the social context of speech, wishes to pursue 'discourse analysis'. The fundamental problem of this 'is to show how one utterance follows another in a rational, rule-governed manner – in other words, how we understand coherent discourse' (p. 22). 'Eventually, the exploration of discourse rules will reach a quantitative phase when variable rules may be constructed ...', constrained by socio-economic class, speaker–listener statuses and the form of preceding utterances. 'But our present knowledge is too fragmentary to make such attempts fruitful. Quantitative research implies that one knows what to count ...' However, 'by the time the analyst knows what to count, the problem is practically solved'. With that degree of puristic unwillingness to pronounce, we shall all be dead before we sin. Bernstein and Lawton in this spirit are arraigned for their sin of the superficial index, for they overlook '*what* is being done with a sentence ...' (p. 305). They in their turn might say that dialectician Labov might be less prone to believe that to know anything one must know everything if he launched his data-gathering boat on a more theoretical sea, suspecting that the currents are codes before testing their strength and depth, willing to replot the chart in the face of their experience. The difference between the data squirrel unwilling to order his individually equal acorns, and his relation who will not collect at all until he has fashioned their store (and is reluctant to abandon it even when it proves to be somewhat the wrong shape) is in them and not in the forest.

There aren't enough chairs to sit, anyway

The relevance of all this to education is extreme. The world is not quite yet full of primary teachers who believe that 'working-class children' are doomed to grunt and gesture, but it does contain many classrooms in which *some* children (a minority of all 'working class' and a very few middle class) and some classrooms in which many children enter to find the control regime unfamiliar, including the invitation to exercise guilt-backed autonomy. By and large their teachers tend not to be skilled professionally or interpersonally at diagnosing or providing contexts appropriate to what they bring. How could they be when our consciousness of the problem is, as it were, only minutes old and we have not yet sorted it out in its barest conceptual elements, let alone improved on dismal track-records about translating correct belief into mass practice?

Whether many parents would elect for solutions for their children other than those oriented to the chance of success and mobility in pluralistic society is, to my mind, most doubtful. And the day of the unwitting parent is passing. That teachers have the duty to recognize the pressures upon themselves and children and their place to countervail these in a positively discriminatory sense seems to me to go without saying. A great deal of our talk about talk might lose its object if we had resources and techniques in education to allow children to transcend locality without losing it. Try the changed pressure of classes of twenty. Socio-cultural models (which include language differences as an important element within themselves) of variations in rates of school attainment *have* come to 'perform an important ideological function ... to render opaque those social, economic and political factors which can be shown to influence directly school performance so that the structure of educational provision as we know it is not open to serious political challenge' (Williamson and Byrne, 1973: 49). But they could not provide the basis in ideology unless they had purchase on reality. Our changing class system still outputs wide differences in income, wealth, values, tastes, languages, etc. – call them 'habitus', style of life, class characteristics or whatever: the logical reaction of a liberal instinct is to compensate for differences in the pursuit of greater equality. Halsey and Byrne and Williamson, among others, are right in suggesting that such pursuit, properly conducted, entails more than extra resources for EPA classrooms, important though resources are.

174

Changing class structures is not within the unaided powers of any school system, but as Hymes (1972) suggests '... demanding that all children have access to universalistic meanings of the "elaborated code"' argues 'for a revolution in power relationships ... not to preserve existing forms of social control and inequality ... but to aid those who are unequal to analyse and transform their situations' (p. xvii). How can this be incompatible with language form and style? The alternative to taking the sting out of some differences is the prospect of having to live without their luxury at all.

So don't rise when I come in

We have a complex agenda of questions and problems for research in connection with the school and social control, rather than a way of evaluating how we do it when we do. Perhaps what we most need to grasp is that so many of our problems of educating *en masse* are new that looking for good solutions from historical or other contemporary cultural practice is bound to prove depressing. Perhaps we currently assume all too readily that as well as at the level of the superfices of control, for example of time and space and physical order, educational systems are doomed to transmit knowledge itself differentially and exploitatively, either by type or recipient. I would contend that there is real but not inevitable foundation for the latter belief. It is drawn from the joint experience of pluralist societies not yet mature and human (not to say knowing) enough to regard differentiated truth as capable of feasible universal access and from the present prospect of the subjugation of difference in one-legitimate-belief systems. Neither have yet taken the prospect of human knowing to where it might go. Even if we believe that historically social control has rested either on the version of mass ignorance which gives to few a highly differentiated all and to the many little, or the one that gives to everyone the same commonly interpreted something, we know that yet else is possible, not just because it has been said but because it has the potential power of being in a universal interest. Knowledge is power because it is good and the good is not singular.

References and name index

The numbers in italics after each entry refer to page numbers in this book

Althusser, L. (1971) Ideology and ideological state apparatuses. In *Lenin and Philosophy and Other Essays*. London: New Left Books. Reprinted in B. R. Cosin (ed.) 1972, 242–80. *100–2*

Banks, O. (1955) *Parity and Prestige in English Secondary Education*. London: Routledge & Kegan Paul. *59*

Banks, O. and Finlayson, D. (1973) *Success and Failure in the Secondary School*. London: Methuen. *153*

Bantock, G. H. (1965) *Education and Values: Essays in the Theory of Education*. London: Faber & Faber.

Barker–Lunn, J. (1973) *Streaming in the Primary School*. Slough: NFER. *159*

Barnes, D. (1971) Language and Learning in the Classroom. *Journal of Curriculum Studies* 3, 1: 27–37. *169*

Barnes, D., Britton, J. and Rosen, H. (1971) *Language, the Learner and the School*. Harmondsworth: Penguin. *169*

Bartholomew, J. (1974) *Sustaining hierarchy through teaching and research.* In M. Flude and J. Ahier (eds) 1974. *144*

Becker, H. S. (1967) Whose side are we on? *Social Problems 14*, 3: 239–47. *35*

Becker, H. S. (1971) *Sociological Work, Method and Substance.* Harmondsworth: Allen Lane. *35*

Becker, H. S. (1973) Labelling theory reconsidered. In *Outsiders.* New York: The Free Press (revised edition). *34–5*

Becker, H. S., Geer, B. and Hughes, E. C. (1968) *Making the Grade.* New York: Wiley. *34*

Bernbaum, G. (1967) *Social Change and the Schools, 1918–44.* London: Routledge & Kegan Paul. *58*

Bernstein, B. (1971) *Class, Codes and Control. Vol. 1.* London: Routledge & Kegan Paul. *171*

Bernstein, B. (1975) *Class, Codes and Control, Vol. 3.* London: Routledge & Kegan Paul. *123–33, 142, 151*

Bernstein, B. and Davies, B. (1969) Some sociological comments on Plowden. In R. S. Peters (ed.) *Perspectives on Plowden.* London: Routledge & Kegan Paul. *138*

Bohannan, P. (1960) *Conscience collective* and culture. In K. H. Wolff (ed.) *Emile Durkheim, 1858–1917.* Ohio State University Press, 77–96. *26*

Bourdieu, P. (1966) The school as a conservative force: scholastic and cultural inequalities. Reprinted in S. J. Eggleston (ed.) 1974, 32–46. *135–7*

Bourdieu, P. (1967) Systems of education and systems of thought. Reprinted in M. F. D. Young (ed.) 1971, 189–207. *134*

Bourdieu, P. (1968) Intellectual field and creative project. Reprinted in M. F. D. Young (ed.) 1971, 161–88. *134, 138*

Bourdieu, P. (1971) The thinkable and unthinkable. *Times Literary Supplement*, 15.10.1971, 1255–6. *133.*

Bourdieu, P. (1973) Cultural reproduction and social reproduction. In R. Brown (ed.) 1973, 71–112. *137*

Bourdieu, P. and de Saint-Martin, M. (1970) Scholastic excellence and the values of the educational system. Reprinted in S. J. Eggleston (ed.) 1974. *135*

Bowles, S. (1969) *Planning Educational Systems for Economic Growth, Harvard Econ. Studies, Vol. 133.* Cambridge, Mass.: Harvard University Press. *82*

Bowles, S. (1975) Unequal education and the reproduction of the social division of labour. In M. Carnoy (ed.) 1975, 38–66. *85*

Bowles, S. and Gintis, H. (1973) IQ in the US class structure. *Social Policy* (Jan./Feb.), 7. Reprinted in A. Gartner *et al.* (1974) *The New Assault on Equality.* New York: Harper & Row. *84*

Brandis, W. and Young, D. (1967) Two types of streaming and their probable application in comprehensive schools. *ULIE Bulletin.* (N.S.) Aug. 1967. Reprinted in B. R. Cosin *et al.*, 1971. *153*

Brookover, W. B. and Pallerson, A. (1962) *Self Concept of Ability and School Achievement.* Michigan State University Press. *161*

Brown, R. (ed.) (1973) *Knowledge, Education and Cultural Change.* London: Tavistock.

Callahan, R. E. (1962) *Education and the Cult of Efficiency.* Chicago University Press. (Phoenix Books, 1964). *71–3, 76*

Carlson, O. (1964) Environmental constraints and organizational consequences: the public school and its clients. In D. E. Griffiths (ed.) *Behavioural Science and Educational Administration.* Chicago: National Society for the Study of Education Yearbook, Part II, 262–76. *65*

Carnoy, M. (1974) *Education as Cutural Imperialism.* New York: David McKay. *83, 84*

Carnoy, M. (ed.) (1975) *Schooling in a Corporate Society: The Political Economy of Education in America* (2nd edn) New York: David McKay.

Cave, R. (ed.) (1976) *The Disruptive Child in the Secondary School.* London: Ward Lock. *64*

Cicourel, A. (1968) *The Social Organization of Juvenile Justice.* New York: Wiley. *39, 43*

Cicourel, A. (1970) Basic and normative rules in the negotiation of status and role. In H. P. Dreitzel (ed.) 1970, 4–45. *45*

Cicourel, A. (1971) The acquisition of social structure: toward a developmental sociology of language and meaning. In J. D. Douglas (ed.) *Understanding Everyday Life.* London: Routledge & Kegan Paul, 136–68. *44–6*

Cicourel, A. and Kitsuse, J. (1963) *The Educational Decision Makers.* Indianapolis: Bobbs–Merrill. *43, 150–2, 154*

Clark, B. R. (1961) The 'cooling out' function of higher education. In Halsey *et al.,* 1961, 513–23. *116*

Clark, B. R. (1964) The sociology of education. In R. E. L. Faris (ed.) *A Handbook of Sociology.* Chicago: Rand McNally. *49*

Coleman, J. S. (1961) *The Adolescent Society*. New York: Free Press. *148–50*

Coser, L. A. and Rosenberg, B. (eds) (1969) *Sociological Theory: A Book of Readings* (3rd edn) London: Collier-Macmillan.

Cosin, B. R. (ed.) (1972) *Education: Structure and Society*. Harmondsworth: Penguin, and Open University Press.

Cosin, B. R. *et al.* (eds) (1971) *School and Society. A Sociological Reader*, London: Routledge & Kegan Paul, and Open University Press.

Cooley, C. H. (1930) *Sociological Theory and Social Research*. New York: Henry Holt. *31–2*

Cremin, L. A. (1961) *The Transformation of the School: Progressivism in American Education, 1876–1957*. New York: Knopf. *76*

Dahrendorf, R. (1958) Out of Utopia. *American Journal of Sociology 64*, 2 (Sept.). Reprinted in L. A. Coser and B. Rosenberg (eds) 1969. *38*

Dale, R. (1972) The culture of the school. *School and Society: A Second Level Course*, Units 3–4. Bletchley: Open University Press. *156*

Dale, R. (1973) Phenomenological perspectives and the sociology of the school. *Educational Review 25*, 3: 175–89. *156–7*

Dale, R. R. (1974) *Mixed or single-sex school?* Vol. 3. London: Routledge & Kegan Paul (Vol. 1. 1969; Vol. 2. 1971). *107*

Davies, I. (1971) The management of knowledge: a critique of the use of typologies in educational sociology. In E. Hopper (ed.) 1971, 111–38. Also in M. F. D. Young (ed.) 1971 and R. Brown (ed.) 1973. Earlier version in *Sociology 4*, 1 (Jan.) 1970. *117–18*

Davies, W. B. (1973a) It depends on what you mean by aims. *London Educational Review 3*, 2: 21–8. *36*

Davies, W. B. (1973b) On the contribution of organizational analysis to the study of educational institutions. In R. Brown (ed.) 1973, 249–95. *140*

Davies, W. B. (1976) Piggies in the middle: or who sir, me sir? no not me sir. In R. Cave (ed.) 1976. *65*

Davis, K. (1966) *Human Society*, New York: Macmillan. *38*

Dawe, A. (1970) The two sociologies. *British Journal of Sociology 21*, 2: 208–18. *18*

Douglas, J. D. (ed.) (1971) Understanding everyday life. Ch. 1 in his *Understanding Everyday Life*. London: Routledge & Kegan Paul. *42*

Dreeben, R. (1968) *On What is Learned in School*. New York: Addison–Wesley. *121–2*

Dreitzel, H. P. (ed.) (1970) *Recent Sociology No. 2. Patterns of Communicative Behaviour*. New York: Macmillan; London: Collier–Macmillan.

Dreitzel, H. P. (ed.) (1973) *Recent Sociology No. 5. Childhood and Socialization*. London: Collier–Macmillan. *46*

Durkheim, E. (1933) *The Division of Labour in Society*. New York: Macmillan (Free Press paperback, 1964). *25*

Durkheim. E. (1956) *Education and Sociology*. New York: Free Press. *30, 93–7*

Durkheim, E. (1961) *Moral Education*, edited by E. K. Wilson. New York: Free Press. *93–7*

Durkheim, E. (1968) *The Elementary Forms of the Religious Life*. London: George Allen & Unwin. *29, 98*

Durkheim, E. (forthcoming) *The Evolution of Education Theory in France*. London: Routledge & Kegan Paul. *88–93, 98*

Eggleston, S. J. (ed.) (1974) *Contemporary Research in the Sociology of Education*. London: Methuen.

Esland, G., Dale, R. and Sadler, J. (1972) The social organisation of teaching and learning. *School and Society: A Second Level Course*. Bletchley: Open University Press. *143*

Everett, H. P. (1937) Control, Social. *Encyc. of the Social Sciences*, Vol. 3. New York: Macmillan. *14*

Farberman, H. A. (1973) Mannheim, Cooley and Mead: toward a social theory of mentality. In G. Remmling (ed.) *Towards the Sociology of Knowledge*. London: Routledge & Kegan Paul. *32–3*

Fauconnet, P. (1956) Introduction to the original edition: Durkheim's pedagogical work. In E. Durkheim, 1956. *29, 96*

Floud, J. and Halsey, A. H. (1961) Introduction. In A. H. Halsey *et al.*, 1–12. *111*

Flude, M. and Ahier, J. (eds) (1974) *Educability, Schools and Ideology*. London: Croom Helm.

Ford, J. (1969) *Social Class and the Comprehensive School*. London: Routledge & Kegan Paul. *114*

Ford, J., Young, D. and Box, S. (1967) Functional autonomy, role distance and social class. In B. R. Cosin *et al.* 1971, 67–73. Reprinted from *British Journal of Sociology 18*, 4, 1967, 370–81. *155*

Freire, P. (1971) *Pedagogy of the Oppressed*. New York: Herder & Herder. *66, 105*

Friedman, N. L. (1967) Cultural deprivation: a commentary in the sociology of knowledge. *Journal of Educational Thought* 1–2: 88–99. *171*

Garfinkel. H. (1956) Conditions of successful degradation ceremonies. *American Journal of Sociology 61*: 420–4. Reprinted in J. G. Manis and B. N. Meltzer (1967) *Symbolic Interaction: A Reader in Social Psychology*. Boston: Alleyn & Bacon, 205–12. *36*

Garfinkel, H. (1968) The origins of the term 'ethnomethodology'. Reprinted in R. Turner (ed.) (1974) *Ethnomethodology*. Harmondsworth: Penguin. *42*

Geer, B. (1968) Teaching. In *Int. Encycl. Soc. Sciences*, Vol. 15. New York: Macmillan, 560–5. *152*

Giglioli, P. P. (ed.) (1972) *Language and Social Context*. Harmondsworth: Penguin. *44*

Gintis, H. (1970) The new working class and revolutionary youth. *Socialist Revolution 1* (May): 13–43. Reprinted in M. Carnoy (ed.) 1975, 310–39. *80–1*

Gintis, H. (1972a) Toward a political economy of education: a radical critique of Ivan Illich's *Deschooling Society*. *Harvard Educational Review 42*, 1: 70–96. *81*

Gintis, H. (1972b) Consumer behaviour and the concept of sovereignty. *American Economic Review 62*, 2. *Papers and Proceedings*, 267–78. *79*

Glass, D. V. (1961) Education and social change in modern England. In A. H. Halsey, J. Floud and C. A. Anderson (eds) 1961, 391–413 *59–60*

Goffman, E. (1959) *The Presentation of the Self in Everyday Life*. Garden City: Doubleday. *34*

Goffman, E. (1961) *Asylums*. Garden City: Doubleday. *34, 145*

Goldmann, L. (1968) *Human Sciences and Philosophy*. London: Cape. *40*

Goodacre, E. J. (1971) Teachers and their pupils' home background. In B. R. Cosin *et al.* (eds) 9–15. Reprinted from *Teachers and Pupils' Home Background*. Slough: NFER (1968). *158–9*

Goodman, P. (1956) *Growing Up Absurd*. New York: Random House. *65*

Gordon, C. W. (1957) *The Social System of the High School*. Glencoe, Ill.: Free Press. *148*

Gorman, R. A. (1975) Alfred Schutz – an exposition and a critique. *British Journal of Sociology 26*, March, 1–19. *41*

Gouldner, A. W. (1954) *Patterns of Industrial Bureaucracy*. New York: Free Press. *152*

Gramsci, A. (1971) *Selections from the Prison Notebooks.* London: Lawrence & Wishart. *102–3*

Habermas, J. (1970) Towards a theory of communicative competence. In H. P. Dreitzel (ed.) 1970, 115–48. *104*

Halsey, A. H. (ed.) (1972) *Educational Priority, Vol. 1: EPA Problems and Policies.* London: HMSO. *174*

Halsey, A. H., Floud, J. and Anderson, C. A. (eds) (1961) *Education, Economy and Society.* New York: Free Press. *111*

Hargreaves, D. H. (1967) *Social Relations in a Secondary School.* London: Routledge & Kegan Paul. *151–2*

Henry, J. (1955a) Culture, education and communications theory. In G. Spindler (ed.) *Education and Anthropology.* Stanford University Press, 188–207. *161*

Henry, J. (1955b) Docility, or giving teacher what she wants. *Journal of Social Issues* 2, 33–41. Reprinted in R. R. Bell and H. R. Stub (eds) (1968) *The Sociology of Education: a sourcebook.* Homewood, Ill.: The Dorsey Press (revised edition). *162*

Henry, J. (1966) *Culture Against Man.* London: Tavistock. *162*

Henry, J. (1971) *Essays on Education.* Harmondsworth: Penguin. *66*

Himmelweit, H. T. and Swift, B. (1969) A model for the understanding of the school as a socializing agent. In P. Mussen *et al.* (eds) *Trends and Issues in Developmental Psychology.* New York: Holt, Rinehart & Winston. *153*

Hirschi, T. and Selvin, H. (1967) *Delinquency Research: An Appraisal of Analytic Methods.* New York: Free Press. *35*

Hirst, P. H. and Peters, R. S. (1970) *The Logic of Education.* London: Routledge & Kegan Paul. *50*

Hirst, P. Q. (1975) *Durkheim, Barnard and Epistemology.* London: Routledge & Kegan Paul. *16*

Holt, J. (1964) *How Children Fail.* London: Pitman. *65*

Hopper, E. (ed.) (1971) *Readings in the Theory of Education Systems.* London: Hutchinson University Library. *115–6, 156*

Hymes, D. (1972) Introduction, in C. B. Cazden, V. P. John and D. Hymes (eds) *Functions of Language in the Classroom.* Columbia: Teachers College Press. *175*

Illich, I. (1971) *Deschooling Society.* London: Calder & Boyars. *61, 65–6*

Inkeles, A. (1966) A note on social structure and the socialization of competence. *Harvard Educational Review 36,* 3: 265–84. *80*

Jackson, P. W. (1968) *Life in Classrooms*. New York: Holt, Rinehart & Winston. *66, 161–2, 172*

Jarvie, I. (1972) *Concepts and Society*. London: Routledge & Kegan Paul. *20*

Jay, M. (1974) *The Dialectical Imagination*. London: Heineman. *99*

Jencks, C. *et al.* (1972) *Inequality. A Reassessment of the Effect of Family and Schooling in America*. London: Allen Lane. *84*

Jensen, A. R. (1969) How much can we boost IQ and scholastic achievement? *Harvard Educational Review 39*, I: 1–123. *78, 172*

Johnson. H. M. (1961) *Sociology: A Systematic Introduction*. London: Routledge & Kegan Paul. *38*

Jones, K. (1973) Women's education. *Education, Economy and Politics: A Third Level Course, Block 5. Case Studies 3–4*, 89–164. Bletchley: Open University Press. *107*

Karier, C. J. (1972) Testing for order and control in the corporate state. *Educational Theory 22*, 2: 154–80. *77–8*

Katz, M. B. (1971) *Class, Bureaucracy and Schools*. New York: Praeger. *68–71, 76*

Keddie, N. (1971) Classroom knowledge in M. F. D. Young (ed.) 1971. *166–9*

Kennett, J. (1973) The sociology of Pierre Bourdieu. *Educational Review 25*, 3: 237–48. *134–5, 139*

King, R. A. (1969) *Values and Involvement in a Grammar School*. London: Routledge & Kegan Paul. *152*

Kohn, M. (1959) Social class and parental values. *American Journal of Sociology 56*, 4: 337–51. *85*

Kohn, M. (1959) Social class and the exercise of parental authority. *American Sociological Review 24*, 3: 352–66. *85*

Kozol, J. (1967) *Death at an Early Age*. Boston: Houghton Mifflin. *65*

Labov, W. (1972) The logic of non-standard English *and* The study of language in its social context. In P. P. Giglioli (ed.) 1972, 179–214 and 283–307. *172–3*

Lacey, C. (1970) *Hightown Grammar*. Manchester University Press. *152*

Lambert, R. (1966) The public schools: a sociological introduction. In G. Kalton *The Public School*. London: Longmans. *144*

Lambert, R. J. and Millham, S. (1968) *The Hothouse Society*. London: Weidenfeld & Nicolson. *144*

183

Lambert, R., Bullock, R. and Millham, S. (1973) The informal social system. In R. Brown (ed.) 1973, 297–316. *145–6*

Lambert, R., Bullock, R. and Millham, S. (1975) *The Chance of a Lifetime?* London: Weidenfeld & Nicolson. *144*

Lawton, D. (1968) *Language and Social Class.* London: Routledge & Kegan Paul. *173*

Lawton, D. (1975) *Class, Culture and the Curriculum.* London: Routledge & Kegan Paul. *64*

Leach, E. (1970) *Levi-Strauss.* London: Collins (Fontana). *43*

Levitas, M. (1974) *Marxist Perspectives in the Sociology of Education.* London: Routledge & Kegan Paul. *61*

Lewin, K. and Lippitt, R. (1938) An experimental approach to the study of autocracy and democracy: a preliminary note. *Sociometry 1*, 292–300. *158*

Little, A. and Westergaard, J. (1964) The trend of class differentials in educational opportunity in England and Wales, *British Journal of Sociology 15*, 4: 301–16. *61*

Little, K. *et al.* (1973) The developments of state education. *Educational Studies: A Third Level Course. Education, Economy and Politics, Block 2.* Open University Press. *56*

Lukacs, G. (1971) *History and Class Consciousness.* London: Merlin Press. *102*

Lukes, S. (1973) *Emile Durkheim: His Life and Work.* Harmondsworth: Allen Lane. *25–6*

Mackay, R. (1974) Conceptions of childhood and models of socialization. In H. P. Dreitzel (ed.) 1973, 27–43. *46–7*

McLelland, D. (1976) *Marx.* London: Collins (Fontana).

Mannheim, K. (1960) *Ideology and Utopia.* London: Routledge & Kegan Paul. *103–4*

Marshall, T. H. (1961) Social selection in the welfare state. In A. H. Halsey *et al.* 1961, 148–63. *59*

Martindale, D. (1961) *The Nature and Types of Sociological Theory.* London: Routledge & Kegan Paul. *24–5*

Marx, K. (1973) *Grundrisse.* Harmondsworth: Penguin

Matza, D. (1964) *Delinquency and Drift.* New York: Wiley. *34–5*

Matza, D. (1969) *Becoming Deviant.* Englewood Cliffs, N.J.: Prentice Hall. *34*

Miller, D. L. (1973) *George Herbert Mead: Self, Language and the World.* Austin: University of Texas Press. *33–4*

Morrison, A. and MacIntyre, D. (1973) *Teachers and Teaching.* Harmondsworth: Penguin. *159*

Musgrove, F. (1964) *Youth and the Social Order.* London:

Routledge & Kegan Paul. *62*

Musgrove, F. (1973) Research on the sociology of the school and of teaching. In W. Taylor (ed.) *Research Perspectives in Education*. London: Routledge & Kegan Paul. *140*

Nash, R. (1973) *Classrooms Observed*. London: Routledge & Kegan Paul. *151, 159–61*

Noel, E. W. (1962) Sponsored and contest mobility in America and England: a rejoinder to Ralph H. Turner. *Comparative Education Review* 6, 2: 148–51. *114*

Parsons, T. (1956) Foreword to Durkheim, E. (1956). *29*

Parsons, T. (1961) The school class as a social system: some of its functions in American society. In A. H. Halsey *et al.* 1961, 434–55. Reprinted from *Harvard Educational Review* 29 (Fall), 1959. *118–121*

Parsons, T. (1966) *Societies. Evolutionary and Comparative Perspectives*. Englewood Cliffs, N.J.: Prentice Hall. *37*

Pitts, J. R. (1968) Social Control. 1. The Concept. *International Encyc. Soc. Sciences*. Vol. 14, 381–95. New York: Macmillan. *24*

Plowden Report (1967) *Children and their Primary Schools*. London: HMSO. *54, 57, 138, 153*

Postman, N. and Weingartner, C. (1971) *Teaching as a Subversive Activity*. Harmondsworth: Penguin. *65*

Reimer, E. (1971) *School is Dead*. Harmondsworth: Penguin. *65*

Richardson, E (1973) *The Teacher, the School and the Task of Management*. London: Heinemann. *141*

Rist, R. (1970) Student social class and teacher expectations: the self-fulfilling prophecy in ghetto education. *Harvard Educational Review* 40, 30: 411–51. *165–9*

Robinson, P. E. D. An ethnography of classrooms. In S. J. Eggleston (ed.) 1974. *168*

Roche, M. (1973) *Phenomenology, Language and the Social Sciences*. London: Routledge & Kegan Paul. *44*

Rosen, H. (1974) Language and class. In D. Holly (ed.) *Education and Domination*. London: Hutchinson (Arrow). *171*

Rosenthal, R. and Jacobson, L. (1968) *Pygmalion in the Classroom*. New York: Holt, Rinehart & Winston. *157–8*

Ross, E. A. (1901) *Social Control*. New York: Macmillan. *24–5*

Sharp, R. and Green, A. G. (1975) *Education and Social Control*. London: Routledge & Kegan Paul. *132, 162–4*

Shipman, M. D. (1971) *Education and Modernization*. London: Faber & Faber. *56–7*

Simon, B. (1960) *Studies in the History of Education 1780–1870*. London: Lawrence & Wishhart. *55*

Smith, D. (1973) Distribution processes and power relations in education systems. *Educational Studies: A Third Level Course. Education, Economy and Politics, Block I*. Open University Press. *116–17*

Snow, R. E. (1969) Unfinished Pygmalion. *Contemporary Psychology 14*, 4: 197–9. *158*

Spring, J. H. (1972) *Education and the Rise of the Corporate State*. Boston: Beacon Press. *73–7*

Sudnow, D. (1965) Normal crimes: sociological features of the penal code in a public defender's office. *Social Problems 12*: 255–76. *39*

Taylor, L., Walton, R. and Young, J. (1973) *The New Criminology*. London: Routledge & Kegan Paul. *35*

Taylor, W. (1963) *The Secondary Modern School*. London: Faber & Faber. *64*

Times Higher Educational Supplement (1975) Servants or Masters? How the civil servants rule British education. Text of OECD Report on Britain, 9 May, 8–11. *53*

Turner, B. (ed.) (1974) *Truancy*. London: Ward Lock. *64*

Turner, R. (1961) Modes of social ascent through education: sponsored and contest mobility. In A. H. Halsey *et al.* 1961, 121–39. Also in E. Hopper (ed.) 1971, 71–90. Reprinted from *American Sociological Review 25*, 5, 1960. *112–15, 150*

Turner, R. (1964) *The Social Context of Ambition*. San Francisco: Chandler. *113–14*

Walker, R. and Adelman, C. (1975) *A Guide to Classroom Observation*. London: Methuen. *170*

Waller, W. (1932) *The Sociology of Teaching*. New York: Wiley. *148*

Wardle, D. (1974) *The Rise of the Schooled Society*. London: Routledge & Kegan Paul. *55–8, 61–3*

Weber, M. (1951) *Essays in Sociology*, edited by H. Gerth and C. W. Mills. London: Routledge & Kegan Paul. *110–11*

Werthman, D. (1971) Delinquents in schools. In B. R. Cosin *et al.* 1971, 39–48. Reprinted from *Berkeley Journal of Sociology 8*, 1: 39–60, 1963. *152*

Wheeler, S. (1966) The structure of formally organized socialization settings. In O. G. Brim and S. Wheeler, *Socialization After Childhood: Two Essays*. New York: Wiley. *151*

White, J. (1975) The end of the compulsory curriculum. *Doris Lee Lectures*. London: University of London Press. *57*

Whitty, G. (1974) Sociology and the problem of radical educational change. In M Flude and J. Ahier, 1974. *104*

Whitty, G. and Young, M. (1975) The politics of school knowledge. *Times Ed. Supp.* 9 May. *144*

Williams, R. (1961) *The Long Revolution.* London: Chatto & Windus. *103*

Williamson, B. and Byrne, D. (1973) Research, theory and policy in education: some notes on a self-sustaining system. *Education, Economy and Politics: A Third Level Course, Block 5, Case Studies 1–2.* Bletchley: Open University Press, 45–94. *174*

Wilson E. K. (1961) Editor's Introduction to E. Durkheim, 1961.

Wilson, T. P. (1971) Normative and interpretive paradigms in sociology. In J. D. Douglas (ed.) *Understanding Everyday Life,* Routledge & Kegan Paul. *19*

Winch, P. (1958) *The Idea of a Social Science.* London: Routledge & Kegan Paul. *16*

Wrong, D. (1961) The oversocialized conception of man in modern sociology. *American Sociological Review 26,* 2: 183–93. Reprinted in L. A. Coser and B. Rosenberg (eds) 1969. *38*

Young, M. F. D. (1971) (ed.) *Knowledge and Control* London: Collier–Macmillan. *64*

Young, M. F. D. (1972) On the politics of educational knowledge: some preliminary considerations with particular reference to the Schools Council. *Economy and Society, 1,* 2: 194–215. Reprinted in Bell *et al.* (1973) *Education in Great Britain and Ireland. A Source Book.* London: Routledge & Kegan Paul and the Open University Press, 70–81. *54*

Young, M. F. D. (1975) Curriculum change: limits and possibilities. *Educational Studies 1,* 2: 129–38. *65, 106–7*

Subject index

189